THE GREAT CRESCENTA VALLEY FLOOD

NEW YEAR'S DAY 1934

To John — a good read! Art Cobery

ART COBERY

WITH MIKE AND PAM LAWLER

Charleston H London

THE
History
PRESS

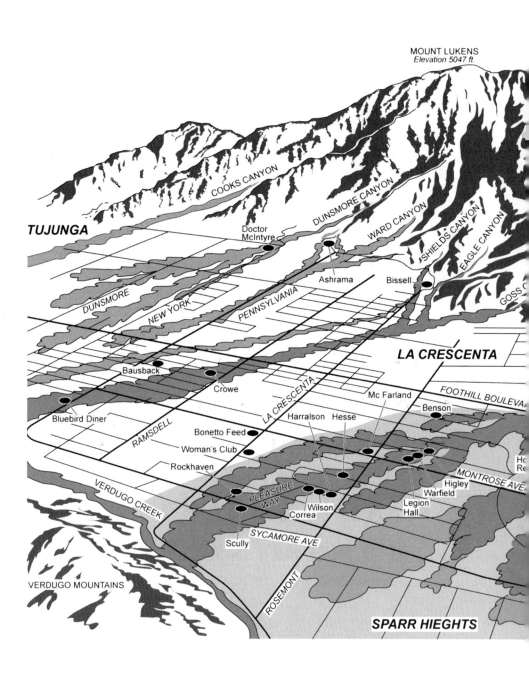

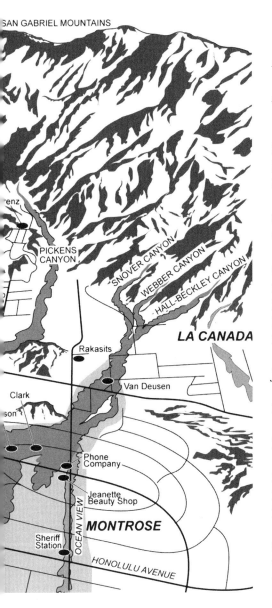

SAN GABRIEL MOUNTAINS

enz

PICKENS
CANYON

SNOVER CANYON

WEBBER CANYON

HALL-BECKLEY CANYON

LA CANADA

Rakasits

Van Deusen

Clark

son

Phone
Company

Jeanette
Beauty Shop

MONTROSE

OCEAN VIEW

Sheriff
Station

HONOLULU AVENUE

CURRENT ADDRESSES OF
SITES ON THE MAP:

Ananda Ashrama—5301 Pennsylvania
    Avenue
American Legion Hall—2537 Fairway
    Avenue (relocated to 4011 La
    Crescenta Avenue)
Bausback—3121 Evelyn Avenue
Benson—2533 Prospect Avenue
Bluebird Diner—3971 Pennsylvania
    Avenue
Correa—3934 Pleasure Way
Crescenta Telephone Exchange—4111
    Ocean View Boulevard
Crowe—3023 Prospect Avenue
Harralson—2624 Piedmont Avenue
Hesse—2631 Manhattan Avenue
Higley—2547 Encinal Avenue
Holy Redeemer Catholic
    Church—2411 Montrose Avenue
Jeanette's Beauty Shop—2304
    Montrose Avenue
La Crescenta Sheriff Station—3809
    Ocean View Boulevard
La Crescenta Woman's Club—4004 La
    Crescenta Avenue
McFarland—2613 Montrose Avenue
Rakasits—2270 Cross Street
Rockhaven Sanitarium—2713
    Honolulu Avenue
Scully—2670 Honolulu Avenue
Warfield—2561 Mayfield Avenue
Wilson—2636 Piedmont Avenue

Published by The History Press
Charleston, SC 29403
www.historypress.net

Copyright © 2012 by Art Cobery
All rights reserved

All photos courtesy of the Glendale Central Library and the Historical Society of the
Crescenta Valley unless otherwise noted.

First published 2012

Manufactured in the United States

ISBN 978.1.60949.449.0

Library of Congress CIP data applied for.

We dedicate this small book to old and young alike who perished in the New Year's Flood of 1934, with the hope that those who continue to live on the sloping mantle of the San Gabriel Mountains remember that history has a tendency to repeat itself.

Kind friend do you remember,
On that fatal New Year's night?
The light of old Los Angeles,
Was a flickering oh so bright.
A cloudburst hit the mountains,
It swept away our homes.
And a hundred lives was taken,
In that fatal New Year's flood.

—*Woody Guthrie*

CONTENTS

PROLOGUE

About midnight, December 31, 1933, a resident of Montrose was helping to free several automobiles along Foothill Boulevard that had been caught in the debris and wash of run-off waters from a day-long rain. The resident paused in his difficult task, wiped rain from his eyes and face, and then froze in his tracks. From up the canyon there roared out of the inky, rain-soaked blackness, a terrible sound. The crashing of boulders and the splintering of huge trees could be distinguished in the cacophony, and above the thunder-like claps could be heard the sickening rasp and gurgle of runaway water.

But in a few seconds, a wall of mud and boulder-laden water 20 feet high struck the boulevard. The resident was pinned by the force of the current against the upstream side of the car he had been trying to free. The car and he were carried across the boulevard and held from further plunging by a pipe handrail guarding a culvert crossing. Pressed in an upright position, he felt the flow pass just over his head. When the peak had dropped, debris had settled around his body up to his shoulders.

The 20-foot wall of plunging, debris-laden water flattened out after crossing Foothill into a scythe of destruction, sweeping before it the lives of 39 persons, completely demolishing 198 homes and rendering totally uninhabitable 401 more. Automobiles, garages, roads, bridges, streets, water systems, power lines and other structures fell before the force. Full toll of the destruction can never be known.

—Reprinted from the Crescenta Valley Ledger

1

THE UNIQUE GEOLOGY OF THE SAN GABRIEL MOUNTAINS

In spite of all the marvels the hand of Man has wrought,
He yet stands impotent before the fury of flood and fire,
No matter with what courage these great Forces may be fought,
They leave in their path destruction, inevitable and dire.
—Kate H. Wright (written on January 1, the morning after the flood)

In order to understand what brought about the tragedy of the New Year's Flood of 1934 that devastated La Crescenta and Montrose, some light should be shed on the history and geology of the San Gabriel Mountains, whose southern range towers over these communities. Mount Lukens, at 5,074 feet, is the dominant peak looming over this valley. The complete chain extends over sixty miles, roughly from Newhall Pass eastward to Cajon Pass. At this eastern end, a number of lofty summits reach 8,000 to 9,000 feet. Mount San Antonio ("Old Baldy") surpasses the 10,000-foot figure. For eons, this mountainous block of the earth's crust has been transformed and rearranged by myriad seismic shocks, which help to account for its irregular shape. These are among the most unstable ranges in the world. And yet, as they continue to shed and self-destruct, they are actually rising faster than they are falling. Their walls are precipitous. John McPhee states in his highly respected book *The Control of Nature* that "the slopes average 65 to 75 percent. In numerous places they are vertical." In short, most of the terrain is in an "angle of repose," meaning that the surface rocks and earth are on the verge of plunging down to the canyon bottoms. Meanwhile, loose soil, sand and

This photo of the Crescenta Valley in 1914 is taken from the Verdugo Mountains looking east. The valley is made up of overlapping alluvial fans sloping south, composed of rocks and debris that have sloughed off the decomposing granite of the San Gabriel Mountains. For thousands of years, seasonal floods have roared out of the canyons, each time choosing a new channel and depositing a new load of soil.

small particles are constantly tumbling down the mountainsides, adding to the debris cones at the base. McPhee estimates that on these steepened slopes, "about seven tons disappear from each acre each year." When fires denude the slopes, this shedding increases forty or even sixty fold. These loose crumbs are called ravel and over time leave huge deposits in the dry stream beds just waiting for a storm of such high intensity that this inert mass is mobilized into rumbling, churning debris flows that roar out of the canyons of the San Gabriels, spewing their earthen load of rocks, boulders and mud onto the sloping alluvial fans or *bajadas*. It is part of an age-old process.

Unfortunately, since the late nineteenth century, humans have chosen to build their homes along these bajadas. Historically, decades have been known to pass without a serious threat. These lapses encourage a false sense of security contributing to what some call "collective amnesia." This all came to an abrupt end as the celebrants of the Crescenta Valley prepared to usher in the first minutes of the 1934 New Year. A powerful storm accompanied by several cloud bursts simultaneously released massive debris flows from six deep canyons, inundating the defenseless communities below. The following pages will tell how the diverse working-class population already in the trough of the Great Depression survived, coped and rebuilt their community with safeguards against such future calamities.

2

THE RURAL CHARACTER OF THE CRESCENTA VALLEY IN THE 1930S

It served the community faithfully for nearly a decade, no one knowing that it had been built in the destructive path of the geologically regular flash floods that swept the valley a couple of times each century.
—from a recent article on the American Legion Hall by Mike Lawler

La Crescenta and Montrose are located about twelve miles north of Los Angeles. They stand on a vast alluvial fan formed by debris loads disgorged from the canyons on the south flank of the San Gabriels. The long slope starts at 3,600 feet and descends gradually to a broad and deep wash at the north base of the smaller Verdugo Mountains, two to three miles distant. This natural channel has served as the valley's principal drainage system carrying floodwaters during the rainy season through the gentle gap between the San Rafael Hills and the Verdugo Mountains southward to the Los Angeles River.

The population of the entire valley from Flintridge westward to Highway Highlands was 16,500 in 1929. We do not know precisely the head count for the Crescenta Valley itself, but a reasonable estimate should fall between 8,000 and 10,000. Although the district was semirural, Montrose, in the southeast corner, was a bustling little town catering to a working-class population. Bonetto Feed and Fuel on the southwest corner of Montrose and La Crescenta Avenues provided for those who stabled horses and raised livestock on their property. Those who cultivated orchards, vineyards and gardens found good friends in the Bonetto brothers. There was a church for almost every religious persuasion. Many newcomers sought refuge from the crowds and noise of urban life. From the beginning, it was a popular bedroom community. The salubrious climate and clean air led to the building of a number of sanitariums specializing in lung and asthma care. In 1923, Agnes Richards founded Rockhaven, an upscale facility designed exclusively for women with mental illness. Verdugo Hills Post 288 of the American Legion started with forty-seven members in 1924. It sponsored a Boy Scout Troop, supported school awards programs and participated in almost every community betterment effort. In cooperation with the Los Angeles County Forestry Department, it distributed thousands of small pine trees that were planted by the local children.

Beyond a doubt, the La Crescenta Woman's Club, begun in 1911, was the cultural center of the valley. It consistently lived up to its official objectives of "advancement in all lines of general culture, promotion of the general welfare of the community, and philanthropy work." There were a number of well-attended public elementary schools, but advancement to high school entailed a five-mile trip south to Glendale. A December 1930 *Ledger* article touted the large number of new families moving into the Crescenta Valley: "Considering the average family as having three members, there were 3,015 new residents added to the population figures of the valley during the past year." The writer feared a rental shortage since most were not home buyers. It's likely that the new arrivals were looking for cheaper shelter as the Depression's hardships deepened. A tribute to the open-mindedness of the area is reflected in the ready acceptance of the Vedanta retreat center established on the high slopes of the San Gabriel Mountains in 1923. The colony known as Ananda Ashrama welcomes to this day all diverse religious groups that wish to worship together.

3

ELFIN FORESTS TO
RAGING FIRESTORMS

Nature's Way

*The flames were so close, that as the family fled, Bob's mother had to extinguish
the sparks that were landing on his clothes.*
—from a recent article on the Pickens Canyon fire by Mike Lawler

In the 1870s, even the indomitable John Muir was stymied in his exploration
when he attempted to penetrate the thorny elfin forest that blanketed over
80 percent of the San Gabriel range. This thick mass of brittle foliage is
made up of many species, including scrub oak, yucca, wild lilac and sturdy
manzanita, as well as a wide variety of drought-resistant flora. They provide
a degree of stability by clinging tenaciously to the shifting surface of the
mountainsides. Chaparral is the collective name for these dwarf trees and
impassable scrubs. They grow in the wet winter season storing their moisture
for the long, hot arid summers. Chaparral on the south side of the mountain
is more stunted. The growth on the northern flank is green and lush where
sycamore and oak trees thrive.

Fire poses an extreme danger during the late summer and fall when the
chaparral is tinder dry. On the positive side, burn-offs at more frequent
intervals can control the density of accumulated growth that fuels major
firestorms. During the dry months, chaparral has a high propensity to
literally burst into flames. It is nature's way of rejuvenating and nourishing
plant life. Some seeds germinate only in the aftermath of scorching heat.
Humans are usually the chief culprits behind these ignitions. The danger
to dwellings is greatly intensified when the mighty Santa Ana winds sweep

in from the desert, spreading the flames beyond human control. To this day, veteran firefighters contend that the timber fires of the Pacific Northwest are no match for the viciousness of the chaparral blazes in our Southland. These fierce burn-offs also set the stage for torrential flooding.

There was no government protection from fires in the early days. The sparsely settled valley relied on friends and neighbors to grapple with these emergencies. In 1896, a group of young men and boys rose to the occasion when a fire crossed behind Sister Elsie Peak (Mount Lukens) and managed to creep into the upper reaches of Pickens Canyon. They scrambled up the mountain and contained the flames with shovels and dirt limiting the loss to four hundred acres of brush land near the crest of the slope. The southern slopes above the Crescenta Valley were saved. According to the old-timers, "These slopes had never been burned off since the coming of the white man." The disastrous fire of 1933 would put that legend to rest.

Fighting structural fires was a daunting task often resulting in the destruction of the building. However, intrepid crews lost only two houses in the four years preceding the decade of the '20s.

Forest fires posed the greatest danger and rallied the support of every man, woman and child. In 1916, the founders formed the La Crescenta Improvement Association to address these problems and from this group, in 1923, evolved the Angeles Forest Protective Association, which focused on forest fires. One of the leaders was Harvey S. Bissell, La Crescenta resident and heir apparent to the Bissell Carpet Sweeper fortune. A close ally once said of Bissell that he was the "answer to all things." He and master forester Art Aiken organized the first crew of firefighters from the young men in the valley. Mr. Bissell provided a truck to carry the equipment. The young recruits were quick to turn out when the fire bell resounded at the Bissell Ranch high up on the northern reaches of La Crescenta Avenue. Experienced staff trained the novices, who learned to function as well-coordinated "military units." When absolutely necessary, they recruited extra manpower by setting up roadblocks and inducting every able-bodied man for the duration of the fire. They were signed on and dispatched to the fire lines with a shovel, back pump and other necessary gear to beat down the flames. After their "impressments," they received compensation from the U.S. Forest Services amounting to thirty-five cents for each hour served.

Foothill branches of the AFPA attended collective maneuvers twice a year in various parts of the mountains. Our locals hosted their first rendezvous in October 1926 at the behest of Harvey Bissell, in a stone cabin built for them at Grizzly Flats on the northern slope of Mount Lukens. The weekend

In the 1980s, author Art Cobery visited the remains of the Angeles Forest Protective Association's cabin at Grizzly Flats on the backside of Mount Lukens. It was here that the citizens of the Crescenta Valley were trained in firefighting and forest restoration techniques. The cabin has since been demolished by the Forest Service. *Courtesy of Art Cobery.*

involved lectures, fire suppression drills and reforestation techniques. At the close of day, 125 participants feasted on a grand beef cookout.

The heroic efforts of the Angeles Forest Protective Association were to last for only six years. During that period, they earned a reputation that would endure among the pioneer residents for years to come. Their last stand took place during the firestorm of 1928, when "a hard-fighting crew of shovel and wet-sack men," backed up by a large fire engine, fought valiantly to contain the wind-driven blaze at Foothill Boulevard. Howling gusts eventually carried the flames south into the Verdugo Mountains and on over into Burbank. For years, the great swath that had burned into the Verdugo Hills was a mute reminder of what occurs when the capricious Santa Ana winds hold sway over a blazing elfin forest.

The AFPA disbanded with the heartfelt thanks of the community. From thence forward, the Los Angeles County Forester and Fire Warden Department would assume their duties. In the meantime, La Crescenta formed its own fire protection district financed through property taxes. By 1930, they had built a rock structure just east of Rosemont Avenue and adjacent to St. Luke's Episcopal Church to house their new fire engine and staff.

The charmed life of the south slope directly above the Crescenta Valley came to an end in the late evening of November 21, 1933, when a fire of mysterious origin erupted near the mouth of Pickens Canyon. It would soon become a classic Santa Ana wind-driven inferno. Remember, even the old-timers, dating back to the late nineteenth century, had no recollection of flames having ever intruded on this watershed. Studies show that after three or more decades of protected growth, the bottom half of the thicket becomes dead, dry and even more flammable than the living solvent-laden chaparral above it. This helps to account for the explosive conflagration that followed as gusty, erratic winds spread the fire in every direction simultaneously. There was no quick way to suppress this fuel-driven firestorm as it raged on for another three days, devouring all ground cover in Blanchard, Cooks, Dunsmuir, Shields, Eagle, Pickens and Hall Beckley Canyons.

When the first dense pyric clouds of smoke began to block out the sun, engine companies and pumpers rushed from all sides in a desperate effort to help their beleaguered neighbors save their valuable "residential districts" and prevent flames from sweeping through the nearby towns. They arrived from Flintridge, Altadena, Los Angeles County, Glendale, Pasadena and the city of Los Angeles. The United States Forest Service focused on federal land but extended help to other areas when needed.

It is worth noting that in 1933 the La Crescenta fire station had only a fire captain and two men on duty. Flintridge employed seven trained men. Although the county and nearby cities could deploy substantially more personnel, this roaring inferno was feeding on decades of dead vegetation beneath the chaparral. More boots were needed on the ground.

Fortunately, that urgent need had been fulfilled eight months earlier when President Franklin D. Roosevelt established the Civilian Conservation Corps (CCC) designed to employ jobless young men between the ages of eighteen and twenty-five in public conservation projects. Each received thirty dollars a month for his service, twenty-two of which went home to his family. The CCC proved to be the most popular of the New Deal programs. By mid-summer of 1933, 300,000 men had enrolled and worked under trained military leaders planting trees, building trails and fire roads and fighting forest fires. During the '30s, 47 lost their lives in this dangerous work. The vast majority returned to their homes within a year or so, healthy, disciplined and with a heightened sense of self-worth. According to the Pasadena headquarters of the National Forest Service, "A total of about 1,800 or 1,900 men, nearly all from the CCC," fought the Pickens Fire for its duration in three shifts of 600 each. Hundreds of these young men fought side-by-side with seasoned professionals manning

There were three Civilian Conservation Corps camps in the Crescenta Valley: one high up on the side of Hall-Beckley Canyon, another in the Verdugo Mountains above the Oakmont Golf Course and this one, Tuna Camp, in the far west end of the valley. The site of Tuna Camp is now the Verdugo Hills Golf Course. *Courtesy of Little Landers Historical Society.*

hoses and saving homes. Determined defenders prevented the flames from leaping southward across Foothill Boulevard.

The firefighters received high marks for structure protection, with the exception of seven homes lost in sparsely settled Briggs Terrace, located on a high shelf just west of Pickens Canyon. Earlier in the evening, the small community had been spared when the flames raced northwest and over it toward the Tujunga border and Haines Canyon. Unfortunately, capricious winds reversed themselves, bringing back the firestorm in all its fury. Pioneer resident Bob Lorenz was only eleven years old when the sheriffs ordered a mandatory evacuation of Manzanita Street at 2:00 a.m. He distinctly recalls the family's mad rush to the car as their mother used a wet towel to beat out the hot embers falling on their clothing. Down the street, he noticed Dr. Hyder and his wife frantically pushing their partially repaired car out of the driveway for their long downhill coast to safety below Foothill Boulevard. Young Bob could not know at the time that his family was destined to experience an addendum to this drama on New Year's Eve 1934, when the flood hit the valley before the ashes had a chance to settle.

After incinerating Briggs Terrace, the winds drove the flames northwest a mile through Goss Canyon and over a steep ridge into the four-hundred-

The ruins of a stone house on Briggs Terrace smolders on the morning of November 22, 1933. The fire that had started the evening before in Pickens Canyon had bypassed these homes but later doubled back and claimed several houses. Many residents barely escaped ahead of the fast-moving firestorm.

acre estate of Harvey S. Bissell, renowned patriarch and leading citizen of the Crescenta Valley. The estate, usually referred to as the "High Up Ranch," was located at the extreme north end of La Crescenta Avenue. Sadly, Mr. Bissell lost most of his cherished orchard, pines and ornamental trees that he had cultivated for over twenty years. The damage was estimated at $100,000, a staggering sum during the Depression era.

The beautiful Ananda Ashrama was about a mile directly west of the smoldering Bissell place. This secluded 120-acre Vedanta retreat had forged a strong bond of friendship with the outside community over the years. There was genuine concern for its safety when, at nightfall on November 22, gale-force winds swept the flames out of the upper canyons toward the heart of the Ashrama. Over 170 firefighters, many of them CCC volunteers, waged a night-long offensive keeping the flames at bay.

At sunup on November 23, it appeared that the fire had abated. The good sisters opened the commissary and began serving coffee, potato soup and bread to the small army that had defended the sacred retreat from dusk till

The Ananda Ashrama, a religious retreat, sits on the foothills of the San Gabriels at the top of Pennsylvania Avenue. On the night of November 23, the fire passed over the Ashrama, burning everything around the religious center but not damaging the Ashrama itself. This photo was taken in the late '20s, but the Ananda Ashrama looks exactly like this today—a veritable time capsule. *Courtesy of Ananda Ashrama.*

dawn. The sisters and others thought that perhaps the danger had passed. The seasoned firemen knew better. All afternoon, they prepared for the final assault. Crews were at the ready. Hoses had been attached to large hydrants on upper Pennsylvania Avenue and stretched for a mile around the perimeter of the Ashrama. Several more fire engines were brought up to support this last crucial stand.

At sunset, just as they feared, fifty-mile-per-hour winds propelled the flames down the slopes into their midst. The fire chief directed the sisters to take refuge in the cloister house and cautioned them to close all doors and windows tight. He assigned twenty handpicked men to lie on their stomachs around the structure and train their hoses on the walls and windows. Sister Amala described those precarious moments as they huddled together on the floor: "The sheet of flame traveled with great speed. The wind was insane in its velocity, and there was no means of escape, with flames above and on all sides. The heat was terrific and the smoke stifling." Thankfully, the cascade of smoke and cinders passed over them with a roar, leaving their blessed shelter unscathed. Later, the chief came to the door and announced, "The fire has gone over...It was the hand of God that saved you. We had little hope of doing so."

Overnight, the Ashrama had been cut off from the outside world. The view from the valley floor revealed a flame-engulfed landscape. The phone lines were down, preventing all communication with the compound and valiant firefighters. Anxious followers sat in their cars at the barred entrance, awaiting any word from the isolated inhabitants. Rumors spread almost as fast as the wildfire. One newspaper headline declared they were "trapped and beyond rescue." The most sensational story came from Lowell Thomas on his national daily radio newscast reporting that "the entire 'Hindu' community had been wiped out." One must remember that Lowell Thomas was the *voice of certitude* during the 1930s.

Daybreak revealed a new reality. The raging fire had passed. Reminders remained. White ash covered the ground. A heavy odor of smoke hung in the air. Some of the oak trees had been seared, but they would survive. Most of the eucalyptus trees, gardens and vegetation were untouched. Above all, no one perished, and the revered temple escaped with only a few singed eves. Luckily, too, the most important structures, including the cloister, guesthouse, library, barns and cabins, were spared. Even the lowly bee house remained unscathed. Sister Devamata was inspired to write, "Ananda Ashrama stands like an oasis in a desolate expanse, the only verdant spot for miles on the charred and blackened hillsides."

To this day, a key memory in the history of the Ananda Ashrama revolves around its miraculous escape from the raging forest fire of 1933. The good sisters recorded those perilous hours in letters, often calling attention to Philip and Ruth Reihl, lauding the couple's efforts in protecting the Ashrama. On the second day of the fire, they left their unprotected home, breeching the barricades, to come to the aid of their besieged friends. When Ruth was not distributing food and coffee to continuous lines of firefighters, she was tending to the needs of the elderly Sister Devamata, "following her like a shadow, watching over her like an anxious mother." After two firemen were overcome and carried away, Philip Reihl manned the hose on the library roof and extinguished the flames. He was seen all over the Ashrama, soaking the temple, patio and arcade roof. The whole community was elated when they heard that Philip had saved Sister Seva's fabled "Bee Cabin" by wetting it down as the flames licked at its walls. Sister Achala summed it up aptly: "No one worked harder or risked his life more than Philip Reihl. He was right on the front line."

Who could foresee that a little more than a month later, the Reihls would face an even greater ordeal just a few minutes after midnight on New Year's morning in 1934, when a wall of water and rocks would crash through their small cottage on Piedmont Avenue.

If we accept Harvey Bissell's estimate of his property damage at High Up Ranch, he clearly suffered the heaviest loss in the November fire of 1933. However, an even sadder story involved a group of World War I veterans, who, anticipating the legal end to Prohibition, invested their small treasure in a winemaking venture. They leased the large stone Le Mesnager barn at the top of New York Avenue and west of the Ananda Ashrama property line. The lease included the wine vats and barrels. L'Heritage Mountain Vineyards became the name of the new company.

The fermentation process was scheduled to coincide with the formal end of Prohibition when the Twenty-first Amendment would kick in on December 5, 1933. Soon, the vats were filled to the brim with new wine. But time and hope ran out when the Pickens Fire swept out of the canyons, consuming everything but the stone walls. Collapsing vats created a 20,000-gallon cascade of wine as it raced out the doorway, drenching the outside soil. Another 1,500 gallons of brandy added to the woeful spectacle. The monetary loss was estimated at $25,000. Perhaps God thought that the "noble experiment" (Eighteenth Amendment) deserved a little more time. Then again, maybe it's just another triumph for irony.

By the morning of the third day, November 23, residents living well below the fire were beginning to think that the danger had passed. But in the afternoon, the smoldering brush and trees burst into flames and made startling progress to the east and west. In no time, three homes in Fern Canyon on the Tujunga side were destroyed. In addition to this number, a home high up on New York Avenue was burned to the ground. Wednesday night was a long sleepless vigil of terror for many valley-ites. Household valuables had been hastily heaped into their cars, ready for a quick getaway at a moment's notice. Fortunately, the courageous firefighters held the line. A *Ledger* article several days later lauded the efforts of the "CCC Camp Boys," saying, "It would have been impossible to gain any sort of control had it not been for the fact that the fire departments had the CCC forces to draw on." The fire came close to Foothill Boulevard on several occasions but never made the fatal leap across.

During the long struggle to subdue the flames, firefighters and those in need relied heavily on the American Legion Hall for sustenance and safety. Years before, members of the legion post had chosen a secure plot of land on the northeast corner of Rosemont Avenue and Fairway Street to erect this sturdy structure. After its dedication in 1925, it achieved popularity as a civic and social center. In times of crisis, it became the community's bastion of strength. Here, Auxiliary Red Cross workers Myrtle Adams and

The Le Mesnager vineyard barn in Dunsmore Canyon was completely burned, leaving only the stone shell. Tens of thousands of gallons of wine and brandy were being fermented in the barn. The wine casks burned and burst, and here we see the dark stain of the wine that flowed out the door of the barn. That barn was rebuilt and today is the centerpiece of the Deukmejian Wilderness Park.

The American Legion Hall, built in 1925, was located on the north side of Fairway Avenue, just to the east of Rosemont Avenue. It was a community center and, in times of disaster, a refugee center. Here we see several World War I veterans forming a color guard in front of the Legion Hall. *Courtesy of Arthur Voltz.*

Vera De Woody Kahn supervised the first aid program and kitchen, serving countless meals and gallons of coffee. Florence Bonetto and *Ledger* publisher Grace Carpenter were among the notable volunteers on call whenever their services were needed. The Legion Hall was your last refuge when you no longer felt safe in your own home.

4

DESPERATE MEASURES IN THE WAKE OF THE PICKENS FIRE

Just after midnight, the lights went out, and they heard the wall of destruction
rumbling toward them.
—*from John Newcombe's DVD on the history of the Crescenta-Canada Valley,*
Rancho La Canada: Then and Now

O ne can only imagine what it must have been like after the last embers had been extinguished and the dazed citizenry beheld the ashen mountain slopes for the first time. Following decades of sheer luck, the entire south flank of the San Gabriels, from Tujunga in the west to the Arroyo Seco in the east, had finally been completely denuded. Over 4,800 acres of prime watershed had gone up in smoke. Miraculously, no one had perished, and property damage was limited.

But in the aftermath of the fire, a more ominous threat was taking shape, one that would require even more tenacity and grit. This threat emanated from the vast amount of debris matter that had been accumulating in the steep canyons dating back to the middle years of the nineteenth century. Over time, dry erosion consisting of particles and crumbs from the fractured crust, known as ravel, had been tumbling down the mountain, greatly enlarging the unconsolidated mass in the canyon bottoms. After a severe burn, this process might increase as much as sixty fold. However, the most pressing threat was the impending winter rain that could drench the hillsides in a matter of days. Several Pacific storms in succession had the potential to increase soil erosion a thousand fold, forcing the canyons to regurgitate their contents in the form of deadly debris flows. Those homeowners below faced the grim prospect of a merciless onslaught of mud, rocks and multi-ton boulders.

This quandary that beset the inhabitants should have come as no surprise. The pioneers who first settled on this vast alluvial plain had noted the "gigantic boulders strewn over the valley floor," proof positive of the violent floods that had preceded their arrival. The Los Angeles County Flood Control engineers had long been aware of the causal-effect relationship between mountain fires and flooding. Flood control planners suffered a serious setback with the defeat of the 1926 referendum that was put on the ballot to raise taxes for the construction of debris basins and flood channels to protect the vulnerable foothill communities.

At one time, the public had been made aware of the hazards connected with building homes below an unstable mountain front. Be that as it may, with the passage of time, commitment gave way to what some have called "collective amnesia," which evolved into complacency.

In 1927, E.C. Eaton became chief engineer of the Los Angeles County Flood Control District. He was well grounded in his field and, above all, scrupulously honest, often clashing with county board supervisors and private contractors, some of whom were prone to line their pockets with public funds. Between 1927 and 1931, this far-sighted innovator drafted the first comprehensive flood control plan for Los Angeles County. The blueprint called for the construction of dams, stream channels and debris basins covering every large canyon along the sixty-mile range of the San Gabriels. It also called for major construction of levies along the eleven miles of the Los Angeles River. Although brilliant in its conception, a request for $34.7 million from the federal government in grants and loans was rejected in 1933. Of course, at this late date, no amount of government funding could have prevailed against the flooding on New Year's morning 1934. Thanks to the persistence of the Los Angeles Board of Supervisors, President Roosevelt finally allocated the money, eighteen months later, to allow Eaton's dream to become a reality in July 1935.

In the closing days of November, the conscientious Eaton must have been at his wits' end after surveying the enormous loss of almost five thousand acres of protective watershed. The lofty green backdrop of the valley was gone. Only ashened slopes remained lurking over the populated flood plain. The likelihood of December rains was a clear possibility. One could only speculate on the duration and amount. And time was running out.

Eaton tried to allay fears by holding a meeting with the chambers of commerce of Montrose, La Crescenta and Tujunga in the large Crescenta township courtroom. The members were told that three hundred workers, made up primarily of Civilian Conservation Corps "boys," were assigned to build approximately three hundred check dams in the canyons. The *Crescenta Valley Ledger* stated that these rock structures were designed "to hold back the water as it sweeps down the barren mountainsides." This proved to be an overly optimistic prediction to say the least. One experienced leader was designated to supervise ten "boys." Supervisor Jessup was said to be pleased with the modest cost of this project. After all, the federal government provided the CCC labor free of charge, and rocks for construction were plentiful to the extreme.

As a companion measure, the burnt-over area, to quote the *Ledger*, "was to be planted with mustard seed in an effort to set the raw earth and lessen the susceptibility to erosion when the big rains come." No one could have known at the time that these seeds had less than thirty days to take root. It would appear that Mr. Eaton utilized the only preventative measures available to him at the time. He may have realized that the last genuine security advantage had vanished in 1926, when the flood control referendum was rejected by the voters.

This feeble emergency system set forth by the county flood planners in the local paper suggests strongly that they did not fully grasp the enormity of the danger that hung over the Crescenta Valley following the intense November conflagration. In fairness to the decision-makers, there was no precedent in their life experience to prepare them for the multiple canyon debris flows of 1934.

The county emergency plan provided three portable stations to be established at strategic locations in the valley where officers were to be on duty around the clock and, in case of heavy rains, prepared to immediately alert the public to the danger. In addition, one or more patrol cars were assigned to operate continuously during storm periods. Special phone numbers were listed in the local paper. In case of threatened damage, patrol cars would rush to the scene. The chambers of commerce also appointed committees to serve in the event of heavy rains and flooding. They were to patrol the washes and protect life and property.

All told, the foregoing preparations to ward off a potential disaster seem rudimentary to the extreme. For instance, where were the plans for voluntary or mandatory evacuations? There was no discussion about the necessity for decisiveness and speed in the face of heavy Pacific storms as they roll in and pump that moisture onto the denuded mountain slopes. In some cases, minutes, not hours, can determine human survival. And yet, we all know that there are those among us who have the propensity to deny reality, however great the risk.

5

LAND OF CONTRASTS

Droughts and Deluges

They decided to drive up and spend the evening visiting in their old neighborhood.
The night they chose was, unfortunately, New Year's Eve. Unbeknownst to them,
they were headed into a disaster zone again.
—*from a recent article on the New Year's Flood by Mike Lawler*

At this point, a brief overview of certain characteristics unique to the San Gabriels is in order. To begin with, these mountains are in a continuous state of disintegration while at the same time rising faster than they are falling. Despite the fracturing and constant rockslides, engineers have triumphed by surmounting this steepened mass with well-constructed roads and bridges. This, in turn, has made it possible for the Forest Service to fight fires largely fueled by chaparral, among the most flammable vegetation complexes in the world. In the wake of these fiery scourges, only a moonscape remains. At least five years are required to replenish this growth.

Meanwhile, the bare slopes are extremely vulnerable to the winter rains, however mild or torrential the downpour.

Nowadays, visitors and new residents to the Crescenta Valley are surprised or mildly amused when they first come upon the huge empty catch basins and dry flood control channels emanating from the mountain front. The basins are designed to trap rocks and debris discharged from the canyons during heavy storms, allowing the floodwaters to flow unimpeded through the concrete conduits into the Verdugo Wash, which empties into the Los Angeles River. Some newcomers cannot fathom the need for such costly infrastructure capable of trapping thousands of tons of debris and simultaneously harnessing dozens of raging mountain streams. And truth be known, these man-made structures are seldom put to the test. But when, on occasion, a Noah-like storm does vent its wrath, they become essential to our very existence. Without these man-made defenses, today's housing tracts at the mountains' base could face a calamity dwarfing the one that engulfed the sparsely settled valley in 1934.

The usual extended periods of dry weather every year from May through October, part of our semi-arid Mediterranean climate, tends to encourage a false sense of security when it comes to winter's rain clouds. Then, too, winter rains are usually moderate as pronounced by the National Weather Service. "Average annual precipitation for the Los Angeles area is highly variable and terrain-dependent, ranging from twelve inches at the ocean to about twice that in the foothills. At downtown Los Angeles the average seasonal rainfall is 14.77 inches." Compare this with Seattle's average rainfall of 39.00 inches! Weather data reveals that since the Civil War, the region has experienced dry years (less than ten inches) about every thirty years in this order: 1870, 1900, 1930, 1960 and 1990. The driest winter on record in the city of Los Angeles was in 1960–61, when a scant 4.85 inches of rainfall was measured. The greatest number of consecutive days without rain was 219, from February 18 to September 24, 1997. With these "dry" statistics in mind, is it any wonder that the concept of "flooding" ranks low, indeed, among the concerns of foothill dwellers? After all, floods come from a superabundance of uncontrolled water.

This should not leave the impression that the Los Angeles region consistently ranks on par with the Mojave Desert. On the contrary, this is truly a land of contrasts. Paradoxically, within this so-called semi-arid area, some of the most concentrated rainfall ever recorded in the history of the United States has occurred in the nearby San Gabriel Mountains. Storms of such magnitude are by no means annual events, but when they do arrive, they inspire a deeper respect for Noah's diligence in the building of his ark. Heavy flooding is usually separated by a decade or more and receives mention in the early accounts of the Franciscan missionaries in the late eighteenth century. We know that powerful floodwaters changed the course of the Los Angeles River in 1815. During the early 1860s, intense rainfall deluged all of California. Measurable rain drenched the pueblo of Our Lady the Queen of the Angels for thirty-six days. The entire area suffered from flooding and massive mudslides. The National Weather Service points to the years 1883–84 as the wettest in history, with rain gauges registering 38.14 at the civic center. Almost 26.00 inches of rain fell in Los Angeles in February and March 1884. There was a loss of life and a great deal of property damage. Fifty houses were washed away in the flooding. Well into the twentieth century, these capricious weather patterns have helped to define Southern California as a land of contrasts, occasionally described with a dash of hyperbole. For some, our long, hot summers are compared with Dante's *Inferno*, while our winters have been described as Neptune's Playground.

6

FLOODWATERS TRUMP GROWTH

1914

FLOOD PROOF LOTS—In east Montrose. Move, reestablish your home on safer, more beautiful site.
—from a real estate ad in the Crescenta Valley Ledger *just after the flood*

In the first two decades following statehood in 1850, population growth south of the Tehachapi Mountains was slow when compared with that of northern and central California. Southern California was too remote and too rough a frontier to attract settlers or even visitors. The journey was even more precarious for health seekers who had long been attracted to California by the likes of fur trapper Antoine Robidoux, who in 1840 affirmed before a Missouri crowd that there was virtually no sickness there. Others had read Richard Henry Dana's highly influential book, *Two Years Before the Mast*, describing the life of a young seaman in the 1830s whose ship collected hides and tallow from the Franciscan missions along the California coast. He was much taken by the salubrious climate, "free from all manner of disease... and with soil in which corn yields from seventy to eighty fold." By the 1870s, the Southland had become more accessible. It was less beset by bandits and desperados. As transportation and accommodations improved, a "health rush" ensued that proved to be a key dynamic for Southern California's development in the 1870s, '80s and '90s.

Tuberculosis of the lungs, then usually called consumption, was the malady that did most to promote the rush to the land of sunshine and health. Asthmatics and rheumatics also joined this long caravan to a special mecca that offered a cure for whatever ailed them. In many instances, there was a quick recovery usually attributed to the mild temperature and pure air. Seaside towns were thought to be advantageous for asthmatics and the drier interior foothills were preferred by so-called consumptives. As the good news spread, tens of thousands of invalids followed in the footsteps of these newcomers. In due course, rest homes, convalescent facilities and sanitariums multiplied to accommodate the influx of potential patients. Southern California had a limited amount of viable work for convalescents after the white-collar jobs were taken. However, less physical strength proved to be necessary in the orange orchards and vineyards. The ideal agricultural pursuit for the less physically able was beekeeping. In the '70s, beekeeping spread rapidly, especially to the interior southern counties. Apiarists eventually pushed California to first place among states in honey production. The clarion call of the health healers abetted by the railroads and the real estate speculators continued to attract converts through the '80s and '90s. Census reports show the Southern California population at 76,000 in 1880; 221,000 in 1890; and 325,000 in 1900. At least a quarter of those living here in 1900 were a product of the great health rush.

La Crescenta itself was founded by a health seeker in 1881, when Dr. Benjamin B. Briggs and family settled on a terrace of land, later named after him, overlooking the valley. His first wife had died of tuberculosis, and the good doctor vowed to someday find a cure for the crippling disease. Within a few years, he managed to purchase vast tracts of land until his estate encompassed most of present-day La Crescenta. He chose the name "Crescenta" because the mountains formed three series of crescents around his fiefdom.

It was a lonely, secluded existence in the early 1880s for the twelve families that lived and ranched there. Orchards, vineyards and, yes, even beekeeping, gradually took hold. However, it was not the verdant valley that it would become in the twentieth century. They were plagued by drought, fire, flood, wind and isolation. Nor did the abundance of gophers, rabbits, coyotes and rattlesnakes improve their lot in life. Battered wagon roads discouraged casual travel. The locals stayed mainly in the valley for their socializing and recreation. At least they had a nearby store and post office. In 1887, a one-room school was built with a volunteer teacher for twelve students.

It is no wonder that the nephew of Benjamin Briggs failed to reap big profits from the real estate boom when he opened up a large subdivision in 1884. Unlike land south of the Verdugos, his lacked both a nearby railroad and a reliable water source. Sadly, the health craze and the real estate boom of the late nineteenth century did not significantly impact the sleepy ranches north of the Verdugo Mountains.

However, south of the Verdugos, as the twentieth century dawned, residential and commercial construction raced along thanks to Henry Huntington's Pacific Electric network of tracks and the anticipation of a plentiful supply of water from William Mulholland's Owens River Aqueduct, destined for completion in 1913. In short order, new cities emerged. By 1910, Glendale had a population of almost three thousand followed by North Hollywood, Van Nuys and Canoga Park. Unfortunately, these phenomenal building achievements were trumped by a bad case of collective amnesia. No thought whatsoever had been given to the threat of flooding. Memories of the enormous floods of the 1880s were apparently erased. The Flood of 1914 provided a costly reality check. To begin with, the winter of 1913–14 was an "El Nino" season, although in those days few, if anyone, saw the relationship between the periodic warming of ocean currents and very wet winters. Consequently, there were no dire flood warnings sent out in advance of this storm. Another significant factor that was not reckoned with was the vast residential and commercial growth that had taken place between the late nineteenth century and 1914. Thousands of buildings now covered the open space that had once absorbed nature's downpours. Finding no abode in the soil, the excess rainfall swept across the asphalt and concrete on its destructive journey to the Pacific Ocean.

During the Flood of 1914, a number of slopes in the San Gabriel Mountains received almost twenty inches of precipitation. Rivers and streams throughout Los Angeles broke through their banks. Floodwaters from Tujunga and Pacoima Creeks spread across the San Fernando Valley. The Verdugo Wash draining the Crescenta Valley sent its torrent racing southward to an overburdened Los Angeles River then carrying a flow equal to that of the mighty Colorado. Nineteen inches of rain in one storm would normally constitute a full season's quota in La Crescenta. Heavy rain and flooding were reported at the time, but the valley seemed able to fend for itself. After all, human development over the years had remained minimal. Then, too, the thick blanket of chaparral had kept the slopes in place while the natural drainage system of gullies and streambeds dealt with the overflow along the bajada.

Even more remarkable, fifteen miles below, the city of Los Angeles was spared, thanks to the sturdy railroad levees that kept the raging Los Angeles River at bay as it passed through. However, south of the city, where the river broke through its channel, there was destruction beyond belief. When the waters receded, the new river channel had moved a mile westward, and Long Beach was a virtual island. Over two dozen bridges were washed out, and more than one hundred miles of roads and highways were destroyed. The river had disgorged millions of square yards of silt into the Los Angeles and Long Beach Harbors, making them unnavigable for months.

Blake Gumprecht, in his classic book, *The Los Angeles River*, summed it up most aptly when he wrote: "Given all the new developments since the great floods of the 1880s, it is hardly surprising that the flood of 1914, while not the most intense in terms of rainfall, or land area inundated, was the most damaging in history. Miraculously, no humans were killed." At first glance, one might think that the above assessment of the causal factors behind the flood was shared by all of the citizenry. This was not the case. According to the *Los Angeles Times*, "The flood was wholly unexpected. Even those most familiar with rainfall and topography of the country never had reason to think that so destructive a torrent could come rolling down from the hills." Supposedly, it was a singular event, resembling some sort of aberration that's not likely to ever occur again. The *Los Angeles Times*, like other prognosticators of the day, had a problem confronting the truth. In retrospect, it is clear that those in power yielded to pressures from developers at the expense of public safety. County weather records were readily available dating back to statehood in 1850. A casual review would have revealed that a number of floods since that date easily surpassed that of 1914. By comparison, the flood in 1889 was a real monster. The evidence was at hand, but not the will to act on it.

In due time, the fog of denial did clear, and the residents came to grasp the full magnitude of the disaster. It became a loud wakeup call for the business interests and the burgeoning suburbs to step up and control the runoff and harness the marauding streams and rivers.

Their initial plans did not measure up to either controlling or curbing future flood threats. Some proposals were unrealistic; others were far-fetched. After months of rankling discord, a flood control bill emerged from the state legislature, signed by the governor, giving birth to the first Los Angeles County Flood Control District in June 1915. Since the floods originated in the mountains, miles away, and thence flowed downward to the sea, it was determined that a uniform assessment be enacted whereby the entire county shouldered the financial burden for the common good. The county board of supervisors was put in charge of this agency.

The real shouting and shoving between the supervisors, engineers and general public began once it was time to develop plans dictating where and how the new flood control system should be built. Entering into this mêlée was James W. Reagan, a querulous character, soon to be put in charge of the board of engineers. The initial task of the board was to draft a practical flood control plan that would pass in a county voter referendum. The majority report proposed that the first flood control projects concentrate on upstream problems, including a series of dams in the mountains, as well as some large earthen basins at canyon outlets to spread the floodwaters. The chief was in total disagreement, insisting that these projects take shape outside the mountains. He also clashed with the Army Corps of Engineers over attempts to safeguard the harbor. The interminable delay in putting a plan before the electorate was due in no small part to the stubbornness of Reagan. This internecine warfare dragged on for almost three years until, in January 1917, a revised report was finally approved by the supervisors and became the basis for the bond issue. With Reagan still at the helm, upstream projects were excluded. Most of it was earmarked for the Los Angeles River and harbor diversion. A small portion of the funding was to go to brush clearance in the river channels between Tujunga Canyon and the Arroyo Seco. There was a great deal of opposition to the county's plan, and it passed by the narrowest of margins. Only fifty-one votes out of over sixty-eight thousand separated it from defeat. Even then, U.S. entrance into World War I delayed its implementation until 1921.

Once started, an important diversion of the Los Angeles River was completed preserving the entrance to the Long Beach Harbor. Somehow funds were also found to build dams in the foothills. Devil's Gate Dam above the Rose Bowl was a boost to the Los Angeles River network. Hundreds of smaller check dams were also built in the mountain canyons.

As the first stages of construction were near completion, it was decided in May 1924 to push forth a second bond issue amounting to over $35 million. In order to avoid another cliff-hanger, or possibly a defeat, Chief Engineer Reagan adopted a new persona. Seemingly almost overnight, he reversed his implacable opposition to badly needed mountain projects as if he had suddenly discovered from whence the flood runoff originated that plagued the settled areas below. He also did an about face on conservation by focusing on large dams in the mountains to control and save floodwaters. One of these massive structures would have been built in San Gabriel Canyon and would have been the largest in the world had it ever been completed in the '20s.

In crafting this new bond proposal, the old contrarian practically abandoned his former commitment to improvements in the lowlands. Over 95 percent of the funding was specifically designated for flood control projects in the mountains. The 1924 referendum was enthusiastically embraced by the voters, with over 70 percent casting their ballots for its passage.

At first glance, it appeared that the new bond money would be put to use quickly and the work would progress smoothly. However, the engineers did not factor in the phenomenal growth that continued unabated during the early '20s. In 1914, the entire state's population stood at fewer than three million. The city of Los Angeles alone surpassed San Francisco between 1920 and 1925, when its population doubled to over one million. A spurt in the continuing real estate boom and the popularity of the new-fangled automobile led to a population spread throughout the San Fernando Valley. The newcomers preferred single-family homes to apartments leading to greater land usage. Pacoima and Tujunga Canyons above this area received short shrift when it came to flood control. The plans called for only rudimentary measures, such as the installation of wire fencing to hold earth and rock levees in place. The Los Angeles River near Griffith Park was almost totally neglected, endangering the lives of hundreds of people living along its banks.

As a result, there was public demand for protection in locations that were overlooked in the bond issue of 1924. The new initiative put on the ballot funded almost $26 million for downstream controls, as well as mountain projects to safeguard the San Fernando Valley. A large dam was mandated for the Tujunga Canyon. Badly needed debris basins were to be constructed below the mountain canyons to capture mud and rocks. Concrete flood channels would carry excess water to the Verdugo Wash. This major channel would also be encased in concrete for the two-mile flow through Glendale.

When the drive for voter approval of the 1926 bonds commenced, all hell broke loose over the so-called great dam intended to span San Gabriel Canyon above Azusa. It was to be the centerpiece of Chief Engineer Reagan's master plan. The public outcry put in jeopardy the entire county flood control network that had been envisioned when the engineers drafted plans for the flood control bonds that passed so favorably in 1924. Even the great George Goethals of Panama Canal fame criticized the dam's conservation claims. Other notables challenged the expense, as well as the safety, of so large a structure. The grand jury, too, was on the verge of launching an investigation.

In the shadow of the dam controversy, efforts to pass the 1926 referendum proved fruitless. It failed by a 7 percent margin.

Passage of this measure may not have resolved all the flood control issues in Los Angeles County, but conceivably, the proposed debris basins and reinforced concrete flood channels might have prevented the massive debris flows of New Year's morning 1934 from overwhelming the Crescenta Valley. Had the bond measure of 1926 passed in November of that year, it would have allowed a time frame of over six years to put a protective infrastructure in place. But this was not to be. It reminds one of the poet's lines:

> For of all the sad words of tongue or pen,
> The saddest of all are these: It might have been.

Looking back, it is understandable that the voters rejected the 1926 bond request. Just two years earlier, they had willingly accepted a similar burden. The intense bickering over the construction of the massive San Gabriel Dam didn't help matters. And let's not forget, by 1926 the newcomers outnumbered the old-timers once again. Of course, these new voters had yet to experience a raging flood in our semi-arid land.

Within months of the defeat of the bond measure, James W. Reagan, the man who for twelve years had contributed greatly to the divisiveness and lack of coordination in the Los Angeles County Flood Control Department, tendered his resignation as chief engineer. At this juncture, the board of supervisors was about to fire him anyway. Work on the San Gabriel Dam continued until September 16, 1929, when tons of excavated rocks and dirt accidentally thundered down the mountainside, bringing the enterprise to a permanent halt. From the beginning, contractors had used shoddy materials and grossly over billed the county. One of the supervisors called it the "darkest episode in the history of Los Angeles County government." Decades were to pass before the voters would again approve another flood control bond.

While the County Flood Control District struggled in disarray, the San Fernando Valley continued to overpopulate, losing some of its rural charm. In just two decades, Glendale had surged from a community of a few thousand to a city exceeding sixty thousand. New home seekers began moving north of the Verdugo Mountains to the Crescenta Valley in search of healthful air and a degree of solitude. This migration actually started to arrive prior to the booming '20s when the state sponsored a "Good Road" program providing the financing to pave Foothill Boulevard and Verdugo Road. The small Glendale and Montrose Railway completed in 1913 also contributed to ending the valley's long isolation. In 1922, the *Valley Ledger* made its debut, along with a new sheriff's substation. The Bonetto brothers built their all-important Feed and Fuel store in 1923. Two years later, the La Crescenta Woman's Club was dedicated to providing cultural leadership for the entire community. Shortly thereafter, the veterans of World War I erected their Mission-style American Legion post. Elementary school attendance reached 762 in 1926. Most homeowners enjoyed the amenities of electricity and natural gas, while the more affluent could access their personal telephones. By 1928, a prosperous foothill community had evolved, surpassing 5,000 inhabitants.

As this rapid growth continued in the '20s, the flood control planners became more and more apprehensive about debris flows endangering the defenseless valley. Virtually no flood control projects had been initiated here, and there was no likelihood of this happening in the near future. Flood control engineers lacked legal authority to prevent heedless developers from constructing homes on flood-prone sites.

Enter E.C. Eaton, who was discussed in chapter four in connection with the Pickens Canyon Flood of 1933. He was appointed chief engineer of County Flood Control in 1927, soon after the referendum of 1926 met its untimely end at the ballot box. Unlike the irascible Reagan, he was a man of few words who willingly delegated authority to able subordinates. However, this was a most inopportune time for even a skilled administrator of his ilk to take the reins.

Reckless overbuilding by the private sector, and the haphazard nature of Reagan's construction projects, had returned the district to its 1914 status in terms of flood control. Eaton simply lacked the money to proactively address these problems. He was forced by circumstances beyond his control to concentrate on stop-gap repairs for the remaining years of his tenure. His hopes of building debris basins and flood channels in the Crescenta Valley, although desperately needed, were destined to be postponed for another eight years.

But in the long run, he left us a legacy that has endured to this day. His comprehensive flood plan accepted by the district in 1931, and implemented by the federal government in 1935, followed his belief that "a chain is no stronger than its weakest link."

7

TENUOUS INTERLUDE

1926–1933

I was just a little girl but I remember well the growing premonition I had that week that something terrible was going to happen.
—Eloise Nicholl Benson

Although the prospect of building a long-overdue flood control system for the foothill communities remained in limbo after the demise of the referendum of 1926, daily life and change went on as usual in the bucolic Crescenta Valley. On the evening of November 6, 1928, residents received the news from their own local radio station, KGFH, that Herbert Clark Hoover had won the presidential race. Of course, in those days, the president-elect was required to wait until March 4 to take the oath of office. While the world waited, La Crescenta entered its first—and I might add, last—flower-bedecked float in Pasadena's January Rose Parade. It won third place in its class. Stuart Collins, community leader and energetic real estate promoter, participated in carrying the valley's banner down Colorado Boulevard. On the dark side, on October 29, 1929, less than eight months after Hoover's inauguration, the New York Stock Market crashed, marking the beginning of the worst and longest depression in American history.

The choice for governor of California in 1930, the first year of the Depression, was a Republican known as "Sunny Jim" Rolph, whose main claim to infamy was his approval of a sales tax in 1933 that fell heavily on the poor, since it included food items. Corner grocers were quick to remind customers as they rang up sales that they must take "a penny for Jimmy." In the midst of this misery, friends and neighbors formed the Crescenta Valley Welfare, a strictly local organization run by Father Healy and the Reverend Andy Clark. American Legion Auxiliary member Florence Bonetto was the treasurer. "It was such a wholesome type of thing," she recalled years later. "No one ever knew who the money went to except me, and sometimes they wouldn't even tell me. It was all based on mutual trust and respect." During the '30s, most building came to a standstill. For Sale signs were rampant. Many of the old ranches were divided up and sold, often to flatlanders who could afford rural homes for weekend leisure.

Still, the population saw some increase. The *Ledger* expressed satisfaction over the number of newcomers seeking affordable rentals. Surprisingly, in the summer of 1932, when the American economy was close to rock bottom, the resourceful citizens of the community launched the construction of a fine ten-room junior high school.

However, in the fall, as the general elections neared, it became obvious that most Californians had lost faith in the over-cautious Hoover and the feckless Governor Rolph. Years of drift and deprivation had given the lie to the once popular Republican motto: "Prosperity Is Just Around the Corner." A new Democratic challenger, Franklin Delano Roosevelt, had captured the imagination of the nation. His pledge was a "New Deal for the American People," with emphasis on the "forgotten man." He promised a government as an agency for human welfare and voiced a strong rejection for his opponent's belief in "rugged individualism." It is worth noting that at the Democratic National Nominating Convention in 1932 Roosevelt was on the verge of losing to Al Smith until California and Texas were persuaded to switch their delegate votes ensuring Roosevelt's nomination.

The presidential election results proved that Roosevelt had judged America's mood with precision. He swept the popular vote and carried the electoral votes in forty-two of the forty-eight states. During the four-month interregnum before Roosevelt took office, the Depression deepened, and it was difficult for the president-elect to maintain a façade of neutrality as the sitting president urged him publically to embrace the failed Republican nostrums of the past. Inauguration day finally dawned. Thankfully, this thirty-second president would be the last to endure that interminable wait in a time of national crisis. The Twentieth Amendment, ratified in 1933, provided that the terms of future presidents and vice presidents would begin on January 20 following the general election.

Although it would come too late to prevent the tragic New Year's flood that enveloped the Crescenta Valley in 1934, Roosevelt's First New

Deal (1933–35) came to be a godsend for the future of flood control in Southern California. The Civilian Conservation Corps (CCC), Civil Works Administration (CWA) and Works Progress Administration (WPA) played vital roles in that endeavor. The CCC, created just twenty-seven days into the First New Deal, earned its battle stripes nine months later when its valiant crews spearheaded the containment of the Great Pickens Fire.

8

DECEMBER RAINS

Prelude to Disaster

It was just 12 midnight, New Year's Eve, when Hazel and I bounced out of bed when we were awakened by a terrific roaring like continuous thunder. As I hit the floor my feet struck ice cold water and mud.
—Charles Crowe

The sense of relief and thankfulness must have been enormous for the locals who had assisted in waging a successful defense against the Pickens inferno. The last flames were extinguished on November 24, 1933. Lives and property had been preserved, but the ravages of the blaze left behind bleak reminders for all to gaze upon. Gone was the green protective blanket of vegetation on the mountain front. No one in memory had ever beheld the ashen mass that now hovered above them. They were well into the rainy season, and there was concern about flooding even as the CCC crews constructed wire-meshed rock check dams in the narrow canyons and planted mustard seeds on the denuded slopes.

In all probability, the average family living on the hillsides in La Crescenta had no sense of impending danger. After all, the residents had just triumphed over the conflagration of a lifetime. Surely, Mother Nature would heal the scars of the recent fire and replenish the growth in a timely manner. Most were newcomers who settled here in the booming '20s and had never experienced the likes of a turbulent Southern California flood. And like most working-class Americans, they were struggling through the first year of the Great Depression and hoping for better days ahead.

These check dams were constructed by the CCC in the burnt-over canyons above the Crescenta Valley. Constructed of stones wrapped in wire fencing, they were supposed to "check," or slow down, the water and mud coming out of the canyons. In practice, they didn't slow the debris flows in the least but simply added to the mud flow as it roared down the canyons.

On the other hand, there was ample cause for apprehension among the older professionals in the Los Angeles County Flood Control, some of whom were privy to a report filed by a consulting firm with the board of supervisors in December 1925 warning of the grave flood danger existing in the Crescenta Valley. A faded copy was rediscovered soon after the New Year's Flood of 1934, portions of which were printed in the *Crescenta Valley Ledger*. Without mentioning burned-off mountains, the nine-year-old document stated: "The Crescenta Valley exhibits to an unusual degree, the effects of violent flood action. The whole area ringed about by steep mountains, is boulder strewn virtually down to the main channel, the Verdugo Wash...This is clearly indicative of but one thing—periodic flood discharges of extremely violent matter." The investigators concluded by predicting a change in the future rainfall patterns leading to "storms of increasing violence and destructiveness."

This dire study, coupled with almost five thousand acres of recently scorched mountainside, presented an ominous quandary for engineers whose job it was to protect life and property in the county from the hazards of uncontrolled flooding. Unfortunately, their mission remained undoable as long as voter aversion to funding flood control projects persisted. At best, they could hope for a few more years of moderate rainfall, knowing that, as a rule, ten years is required to get a complete stand of chaparral growth on burned-over ground. At the time, it may have seemed a reasonable hope. The United States Geological Survey published in 1937 confirms that prior to the New Year's Flood of 1934, "The average rainfall in the Crescenta Valley for the last 15 years had been normal, ranging from 22 to 24 inches... Just over the divide, on the headwaters of the San Gabriel River at Opids Camp (altitude 4,250 feet), the average rainfall for the last 15 years had been 38.23 inches (normal for that elevation). For the City of Los Angeles (altitude 417 feet), the average seasonal rainfall for the past 15 years had been 15.00 inches." These statistics were most reassuring for the immediate future.

On December 14 and 15, the barren slopes and valley were treated to four inches of healthy precipitation—just enough to clear the air and dampen the dusty ash on the mountainsides. Indeed, this may have been perceived as a good omen as the valley-ites welcomed the Yule Tide. The previous season's total was a mere 1.67 inches.

Christmas came and departed. Within a week, residents would usher in a new and hopefully more prosperous year. Many planned festive parties with families and friends, culminating in the traditional midnight toast. Others were to turn in early in preparation for the Rose Parade on New

Year's morning. Those who could afford it looked forward to the Rose Bowl game, where Stanford, the hometown favorite, was sure to prevail over the "Eastern imposter," Columbia University.

Cheerful anticipation grew as the great day approached. But on the evening of December 29, a light drizzle enveloped the valley. Was this the harbinger of bad things to come? According to the Swamiji, trusted leader of the Ashrama high on the northwest slope of the valley, "There was nothing to indicate a storm. It was a gentle, steady rainfall." However, the next day, Saturday, December 30, a tropical storm of great magnitude moved in from the northwest. This was a force to be reckoned with. Before it moved on, in less than two days, it would drop at least fourteen inches of rain on the burned-over slopes and wreak havoc and devastation on a defenseless community of almost ten thousand souls.

This proved to be different from many of the previous storms in the region because higher rates of rainfall were concentrated at lower rather than the usual higher altitudes for most of its duration. In the Geological Survey of 1937, looking back, this phenomenon was explained thusly: "The outstanding feature of the storm...was the strong, relatively cool, sustained surface wind, which continued from an easterly direction throughout the rainfall period. Most of the time the wind was from the east or northeast." In short, "Before the moist air reached the slopes of the San Gabriels...it was under run by an unusually cold easterly wind...which increased rainfall over the valley lands and lower foothill regions."

This massive slow-moving storm was loaded with moisture as it stalled over Southern California, drenching it for two full days. Earlier on, it adversely impacted the vicinity of Venice, partially inundating several small communities. But the greatest damage and loss of life was inflicted on the Crescenta Valley, and to a lesser element, Glendale and Burbank. Numerous bodies were discovered in the mud, and several were actually washed out to sea with the wreckage.

By any measure, it was a phenomenal storm. According to the National Weather Service, "Fourteen weather stations recorded maximum two-day rainfalls, with two locations recording 1,000 year events." Flintridge, just east of Montrose, received 14.92 inches, while Azusa tried to absorb 16.29 inches. A rain gauge on the slopes of Mount Wilson measured almost 15.00 inches on New Year's Day.

On Saturday, December 30, dark clouds enveloped the Crescenta Valley, bringing with them the onset of the storm. This was not a drizzler. This was the new reality. And yet, it did not deter a few from driving up the steep hill to the Ananda Ashrama for services. Most remained home hoping to attend on Sunday, December 31, "when the weather cleared." Sunday's dismal dawn brought with it the ominous certainty of heavier rainfall. Surely this would cancel the forthcoming religious celebration. To the surprise of everyone at the Ashrama, twenty-five loyal followers braved the slippery trek up the hill. The rain did not abate while services were held in the temple. Durable Brother George, of the Ashrama, battled the increasing flooding outside in the temple patio. Soon, others, under the direction of the Swamiji, pitched in to divert the erratic waters. Shortly thereafter, Harvey Bissell and two friends made their way over from his besieged estate at the top of La Crescenta Avenue to warn them that Ocean View Avenue was the only passable road in the area.

By noon, the hillside dwellers below were becoming both frustrated and concerned with their plight. The lower valley was absorbing an endless soaking that would test the patience of Job. Nor did there appear to be any respite from this Noah-like event. In fact, at about 2:30 p.m., the moisture-laden clouds began to release even more precipitation, which was destined to continue until the climax of the storm, shortly after midnight on New Year's morn.

From this time on, many homeowners struggled desperately to construct adequate sand bag barriers to protect their property. Hundreds of federal workers from the Civil Works Administration and the Civilian Conservation Corps labored mightily throughout the afternoon, attempting to keep the flow of water, rocks and mud within the surging stream beds. County and city employees worked by their side. At this juncture, damage was largely confined to mud-impacted autos, gravel and silt-filled streets and washed-out yards and gardens.

As evening approached and the New Year was just hours away, most families hunkered down, thankful for the warmth and safety of their sturdy homes. January 1, 1934, was bound to ring in a clear, crisp and cloudless day. Of course, there were those who were not to be dissuaded by the inclement weather. Young people, especially, were determined to brave the wind and rain to go party-hopping with their companions. There were also outsiders who drove up Verdugo Road in the pouring rain to celebrate with one and all the promise of a better New Year. Lastly, there were those with health problems or whose homes were vulnerable to gushing streams and runoff. Fortunately, they had the refuge of the "Gibraltar of the Valley," known as the American Legion Post 288. The Legion Hall traditionally opened its doors in times of crisis. Only a month earlier, the Legion Auxiliary of the Red Cross, led by Myrtle

Adams and Vera De Woody Kahn, had provided shelter and nourishment for hundreds of men who fought the Pickens Fire. To paraphrase the poet Robert Frost: "This is where when you have to go, they have to take you in." Mrs. Adams had been in poor health prior to the storm, and her daughter begged her to stay home, but according to the local paper: "As chairperson of the Auxiliary Red Cross she felt compelled to answer the call of duty." Ironically, when Florence Bonetto called to offer her services that night, Myrtle excused her because she knew that she had guests that weekend. In later years, Florence often recalled that fortuitous phone call that saved her life. Mrs. Kahn was also a loyal Red Cross volunteer, frequently seen by Myrtle's side in the Legion Hall. She lost her husband, Captain Maximillian Kahn, in World War I and came to La Crescenta from Pennsylvania in 1929 to be close to the rector of St. Luke's and his family, whom she had known since childhood.

As the fingers of the clock moved resolutely toward the great ritual that eclipses the old and gives birth to the New Year, the storm persisted, showing no signs of abating. For fifteen years, precipitation had been reasonably consistent in the foothills, averaging twenty-two to twenty-four inches for a typical season. However, this storm was about to exceed fourteen inches in less than two days. At 11:00 p.m., it moved to higher elevation, continuing to pump moisture into the thoroughly soaked hillsides. And then, several minutes before midnight, a short but dramatic transformation took place. For an incredible fifteen minutes, the heavens opened with a vengeance, releasing a deluge that would change the history of the Crescenta Valley forever. Those who lived through it recall a thunderous cloudburst in the mountains that shook the countryside, giving birth to a short, tumultuous shower that simultaneously triggered massive debris flows in every major canyon above the valley.

For decades, the smaller storms that were the norm had failed to dislodge the accumulation of dry ravel, rocks and mixed vegetation that had clogged the base of these channels. Add to this "slope slippage," which frequently deposited swaths of earth, roots and all in the canyon beds.

Finally, a storm of sufficient duration accompanied by an intense event brought the contents of these chasms bursting forth on the valley below. To quote the Geological Survey of 1937: "It was the midnight shower (cloud burst?) climaxing 18 hours of continuous rainfall, that appears to have been the immediate cause of the great flood which did practically all of the damage in the Crescenta Valley."

Although the violent discharges out of the canyons lasted less than twenty minutes, the human cost and property damage were monumental and seemingly endless for those who endured them.

During that short lapse of time, 700,000 cubic yards of soil vacated 7.5 square miles of burned-off mountainside. That is enough sediment to fill 77,777 ten-wheel dump trucks (which is 700,000 ÷ 9 cubic yards per dump truck). And this does not include the debris and silt that passed into the Verdugo Creek on its way to the Pacific Ocean.

These ponderous, wave-like debris flows of rocks, boulders, mud and water swept across the valley in a southwesterly direction, obliterating every human habitation in their path before intersecting with the Verdugo drainage two miles away. This is the natural direction for the mountain runoff to follow. Today's concrete flood channels attest to this, having been built in many of these ancient streambeds.

We may never know the precise death toll. The *Ledger* lists twenty-eight as having perished. My count, including visitors on New Year's Eve, comes to thirty. It is also possible that some homeless people living near the canyon mouths were swept away or buried by debris. The late pioneer resident Charles Bausback felt strongly that these homeless victims were never counted in the final tally of the dead or missing.

The *Ledger* appears to have completed an accurate survey of the property damage in late January 1934. According the their figures, 49 valley homes washed away, 40 were destroyed and 158 damaged.

The above descriptions of the debris flow assaults are cursory, lacking the stark reality and terror experienced by the men, women and children who lost their lives in a matter of seconds or those who fled into the darkness of the storm and survived—some by instinct, others by sheer luck.

The two canyons, Hall Beckley and Pickens, were responsible for the greatest destruction and loss of life. Damage caused by Eagle, Goss, Shields, Dunsmore and Cooks Canyons pales in comparison. (See frontispiece flood map.)

HALL BECKLEY CANYON

Hall Beckley is a deep, steep canyon that originates high above the western border of present-day La Cañada. A drive up colorful Palm Drive will take you partially within its walls. Its steep slopes provide 1.3 square miles of watershed. The canyon was named after two resourceful sheep ranchers and grape growers who settled here in the early 1880s.

The violent discharge of rock, boulders and debris that burst forth from the mouth of this canyon at approximately 12:09 a.m. on New Year's morn followed a decidedly southwestern course, spreading widely as it passed over Cross Street and even wider when reaching Foothill Boulevard.

Although sparsely settled above Foothill, there were a number of homes sufficiently flooded to render them uninhabitable, including the stately Van Deusen home on Castle Road. The Rakisits family, whose home on Cross Street near Ocean View Avenue escaped the wrath of the debris flow, opened their home to dozens of refugees until the overflow of displaced people had to be sheltered in the garage. Not every householder proved to be a Good Samaritan on that dreary night. In January 2008, during a reunion of flood survivors, Eugene Rakisits told how he, along with his father and brother, spent more than an hour digging through mud that had wedged a helpless woman against the foot of a car. She had two broken legs and broken ribs. With great physical effort, the three men carried the badly injured woman

This massive boulder was deposited in the middle of Foothill Boulevard by the Pickens Canyon flow. These boys have made it their grandstand for watching the cleanup activities. The young boy in the middle is Gene Rakasits. Gene, now in his nineties, regularly shares his vast store of memories of the flood with today's generations.

The view looking down Ocean View Boulevard is dismal where the Hall Beckley Canyon flow crossed the road. The cleared area to the right used to be a neighborhood. *Courtesy of Joe and Linda Rakasits.*

to the doorstep of a known doctor, close by, who refused to open his door until the rescuers threatened to break it down. I'm told that in later years, the doctor developed a more compassionate attitude.

Passing over Foothill Boulevard, the debris mass reached Ocean View Avenue and skirted the base of Collins Hill, after which it split into two directions. One extremely heavy load proceeded southwest toward Holy Redeemer Catholic Church, sliding mercilessly through the neighborhoods of West Glenada and Del Mar Avenues. The other half plunged down Ocean View directly into Montrose and beyond.

Fifteen gas company employees barely escaped certain death while they were digging out their truck. They were forced to climb the steep driveway of Collins Hill. There they were given the shelter of the Hill Top Apartments, five men to a room, until 2:30 a.m. No safer protection existed than this unique hill overlooking the ruin below.

The homes on the steep streets of West Glenada and Del Mar were quickly engulfed by two enormous torrents of mud, rock and broken trees, including six homes that were battered off their foundations on West Glenada. The humble home of the Clark family was one of those destroyed by the inexorable pile of swift-moving rubble. The Reverend Andy Clark and his wife, Anna, had

As they had for thousands of years, the seasonal floods coming out of the canyons cut new channels across the alluvial fans of the valley. Unfortunately, by 1933, neighborhoods had been built on those alluvial fans. The new channel that the Hall Beckley Canyon flow chose passed right through this group of houses above Montrose.

been enjoying a rare holiday at Palm Springs when the disaster struck. Their teenage son, Alfred, and his older sister, Eleanor, were alone when the deadly debris flow crashed through the rear of the house. The boy said later that his sister had been instantly killed when an outside door fell, crushing her head. Her limp body was swept from his arms by the heavy waters as he struggled to carry her out the front door. Eleanor was a gifted violinist and member of the Glendale Symphony. Blessed with a beautiful contralto voice, she was the featured vocalist at both civic and religious events. When the parents returned to flood-scarred Montrose, Eleanor's body had yet to be discovered in the wreckage of the Methodist church on Montrose Avenue, Alfred was in the hospital with a broken shoulder and their home and precious possessions were gone. It was a devastating shock for the mother and father. How could such a calamity beset the much-loved Andy Clark? He was known to one and all as the valley's "Good Angel."

One reader of the *Ledger* once commented: "If you see the Rev. Andy Clark starting out late on a windy evening when everyone else is going home to a warm supper and cozy fire, to visit homes where food is needed or where medicine is necessary, you would get some idea of the personal sacrifice he makes in carrying on his work." True to form, "Our Andy" did not grieve

Eleanor Clark's body was found at the base of the Montrose Methodist Church on Montrose Avenue, near Orangedale. Here a group of workers, including her father, Reverend Andy Clark, extricate the body of the young woman from a pile of debris.

long for himself. Within days, he was reaching out to other victims, especially the needy children. Is it any wonder that soon after his passing in 1938, the good citizens renamed La Crescenta Junior High the Anderson W. Clark Junior High School? There were no dissenters. Today, we call it Anderson W. Clark Magnet High School. Once again, no dissenters.

In all accounts of those who personally experienced the flood at about 12:09 a.m., the overburdened streams leaped out of their channels entirely and tore madly across the shortest distances to the bases of the alluvial fans, carrying death and destruction with them. One man on Montrose Avenue, whose property was located safely above the turbulence, witnessed the deluge of what resembled a mass of wet cement laced with rocks and tumbling boulders moving rapidly down Del Mar Avenue. He reported hearing cries from his neighbors as they extricated a man from its sodden clutches. He was startled to see in mid-current the partially demolished four-room home of Mrs. R.H. Johnson floating by. It finally crashed against a telephone pole across from the church on the southwest corner of Orangedale and Montrose Avenue. Of the four homes on Del Mar, her small cottage was the only one to be actually washed away.

This car is almost completely buried and tangled in tree roots.

Looking north up Verdugo Road near the intersection of Glencoe, one can see that even this far south of Montrose a good two feet of mud and rocks have been deposited by the Hall-Beckley flow. In the background is the distinctive Triangle Building at Verdugo and Arlington. It was a popular nightspot, and a banner hanging from it advertises beer, as Prohibition had ended just three weeks earlier.

The next morning, she asked Tob Lamar, the commander of the American Legion, to retrieve her dentures in the bathroom of her wrecked home. This he did, finding them safely nestled in a glass of water by the sink.

Amazingly, it was a small but solid hill of dirt in Mrs. Johnson's backyard that diverted the flow by twenty feet, thus saving Holy Redeemer from a direct hit and extensive damage. This was also fortuitous for the forty refugees who sought shelter in the church that night as guests of Father Patrick Healy.

After crossing Montrose Avenue, these raging flows cut very wide swaths east and west of Orangedale and Florencita. They created a monumental mess of silt, rocks and boulders in the wide intersection where Orangedale joins Honolulu Avenue. Nor were sections of Sparr Heights spared as a flood of debris raced southward to the Verdugo Wash, where it ultimately spent itself.

An incredible story of hope and despair appeared in the *Ledger* early in January describing how Mr. and Mrs. Panzer and children, Jean and Richard, survived in their home at the top of Del Mar, just above the phone company on Ocean View. The north side of their home ripped away in the roaring torrent. They were forced to climb to the roof and cling there as large boulders and small rocks rammed against the walls, making it extremely unsteady. When the worst had passed, they decided to slog down Ocean View to Montrose Avenue, where a neighbor and friend lived on safer ground. As they carefully made their way down through the mud-filled craters, they came upon a little boy, barely breathing. They recognized him as four-year-old Jackie Klass. After working on him for a while, he regained consciousness, and they were able to carry him tenderly to their safe haven.

Sadly, that's not the end of the story. The next day, the body of Betty Lorraine Klass, ten-month-old baby sister of Jackie, was found behind the Jeanette Beauty Shop. Both children were washed from the arms of their parents during the storm. The wrecked beauty shop had belonged to Mrs. Panzer.

Through most of the twentieth century, hard-line telephones were the essence of communication, especially in times of crisis when other modes of reaching people failed. The large rectangular building on the west side of Ocean View Avenue, just below Del Mar, housed the Crescenta Telephone Exchange, which was the basic link to most of the valley and the outside world. Normally, we do not think of telephone operators as heroines, but these valiant women remained on duty, refusing to abandon their posts after being urged to do so as the storm increased in intensity later in the evening. A major debris flow from Hall Beckley Canyon actually flooded part of the office shortly after midnight. Throughout the ordeal, they remained at their switchboards, sending and receiving vital information for rescue operations. Assurance was also given "in calm tones" to many incoherent callers.

During a badly needed break, a Miss McLellan went to look after her car and found that it had washed to the corner of Montrose and Ocean View. The motor would not start, so she released the brake, permitting it to be washed to Honolulu Avenue, where it was to be towed home. According to the young lady, the water was running so fast that she was unable to return to the office. Mr. Thomas, in charge of maintenance, had to battle his way to work, at times wading through waist-deep water. He eventually reached his destination, where he kept the equipment functioning until daybreak.

A group of enterprising amateur radio operators also performed an emergency service by setting up in the Montrose Radio Shop. According to these volunteers, eighty messages were sent and received over two days. The sheriff's office expressed its appreciation.

Eleven days after the flood, teenage brothers Dick and Don Carpenter explored the depths of Hall Beckley Canyon. They were sons of Grace Carpenter, publisher of the *Ledger*, who recorded their observations. They were surprised at the stark changes and devastation in the canyon. They reported tall trees completely sheared off at ten feet. Fourteen rock-wired check dams and a large cement dam were wiped out. Logs had wedged across the cement dam forming a ten-foot-deep lake before it broke. Slope landslides during the storm produced the same outcome. Clearly, new solutions were needed to curb the natural forces of nature.

PICKENS CANYON

The stunning beauty of the deep, wide-sloped Pickens Canyon is revealed to thousands of daily drivers on the 2 Freeway as they approach the interchange going west onto the 210 Freeway. It was named after Theodore Pickens, a colorful but shrewd land speculator, who secured the water rights before establishing a homestead within its walls in 1871.

Pickens Canyon, with its 1.6 square miles of slope, is the largest and deepest in the chain of canyons above the valley. The stream starts below its 4,600-foot divide and travels northeast for half its course before turning southwest a mile or so above Foothill Boulevard. Crossing this thoroughfare, it continues for another two miles before emptying into the Verdugo Wash.

Megatons of sediment and debris had been building up for decades above the 2,800-foot level. It remained trapped there because the smaller storms proved too weak to disburse this ever-growing load onto the older cone, enabling it to break up and meander down the cone naturally, spreading and dissipating its transporting capacity. Instead, the smaller floods carried just enough debris matter to gradually deepen and widen a two-mile-long channel, with some walls as high as 160 feet, that flattened out at 2,100 feet elevation, just above Foothill Boulevard.

The two-day storm had saturated the slopes and canyons to the point that major debris flows were possible if not imminent. The missing ingredient was an intense weather event to trigger them. The short midnight deluge as the New Year began provided that intensity.

The ponderous Pickens debris flow was particularly threatening because, once mobilized, its great mass of pent-up mud and rocks was funneled into a confining channel for two or more miles as it raced pell-mell to Foothill, where it burst forth, cresting at twenty feet. A survivor exclaimed at the time, "It was deafening to hear and maddening to see."

An unknown newspaper carried a New Year's Eve story about a gentleman living off Briggs Avenue and very close to Pickens Canyon who witnessed the peak of the flood close to midnight: "Boulders, many weighing 20 tons or more, rolled down the wash to the accompaniment of the roar of the waters. It shook the house as though it were in the grasp of an earthquake. In fact, more than it did during an earthquake! My cement floor was cracked as the result of the vibration of those boulders as they smashed against each other." The Geological Survey of 1937 has a picture of the west bank of Pickens Canyon at Orange Avenue, about a mile above Foothill. At that point, material from a debris wave passed over the top of this twenty-three-foot bank. Pity any homeowner living above that bank!

W.D. Chawner's Caltech master's thesis on the flood quotes a Pickens Canyon resident who was caught in a debris flow: "About 11:45 on New Year's Eve we heard a dull roar reverberate through the canyon. Before we could get to the porch, a flood of water swept us through—all were carried far down the canyon. Then, from higher ground we watched a wave of water 15 feet high roar through the canyon carrying with it houses, boulders, and people."

No canyon on the south face of the mountains above the Crescenta Valley matched the ferocity or violence of its discharge minutes into the 1934 New

The main flow from Pickens Canyon remained fairly channelized until slammed against and over this pitifully inadequate channel under Foothill Boulevard near Briggs Avenue. This "speed bump" caused the debris flow to spread out laterally as it roared through the neighborhoods below Foothill.

Year. A seventy-ton boulder deposited in the center of Foothill Boulevard attests to this force.

After breaking out of its confined channel at Foothill, the mighty flow flattened and spread rapidly several hundred yards to the east and west. A core of the flow followed the path of its old streambed, overflowing its banks as it traveled relentlessly toward the American Legion Hall and Montrose Avenue. A variety of smaller flows meandered in different directions, spreading mud and silt.

A heavy load moved southwest across Community and Prospect Avenues. Acting capriciously, the fast-moving mass skirted the large two-story Goldstein home on Community and hammered a number of domiciles on the street below. The Benson family, with two young teenagers, were preparing to usher in a quiet New Year at 2533 Prospect Avenue. Eloise, thirteen, and Malcolm, fourteen, were comfortable with their parents' decision to stay at home that night. However, Eloise related that she could

In this view looking north from Prospect Avenue just east of Rosemont, we see the intact Broun house to the left and the intact Goldstein house farther back. In the center is the foundation of a house that has been cleanly sheared off, recognizable only by the front steps that now lead to nothing.

not shake a nagging premonition of imminent danger. The endless rainfall was getting on her nerves. Her brother remembers the flood hitting exactly at midnight because he was boiling water for tea as the teakettle started to whistle at twelve o'clock. Eloise said:

We heard it coming with a very loud roar. We huddled in the dining room looking out the window. Mother knocked over a standing planter and she hastened to clean up the mess. I wondered why—I had a sense that we all would soon be washed away. We watched as the second house to the east of us washed across the street. The house next to us filled up to the window sills with adobe-type mud. Our house was spared because it was just a foot higher than the rest.

Only one home washed away on their block that night, and nine were damaged. In the case of the house next door, "damaged" meant months of arduous labor digging out the hardened mud. The interior was virtually gutted.

Less than a quarter mile downhill from the Bensons lived the Higley family at 2547 Encinal, just east of Rosemont Avenue. The 210 Freeway replaced this stretch of Encinal in 1972. Homer and Ethel Higley were both twenty-seven. They had two children, Lee, eight, and Barbara, six, plus her small dog. The father was worried that evening about the excessive runoff around the house and garage and checked the yard a number of times that evening.

Harold Nuzum, a local attorney, lived next door with his family. For some reason, it was believed that his place was safer. Mr. and Mrs. Aiello, neighbors to the east, thought so and sought refuge there with their two children. The Higley family declined their invitation. "At 12:05 the Nuzums heard the sound of rolling and grinding rocks and hastily went to the front of their home as boulders crashed into the back and the flood waters swept in. Mr. Nuzum, with great presence of mind, opened the front door so the waters might escape." When the floodwaters subsided, the Nuzum and Aiello families made their way through waist-high water and mud to the safety and warmth of a friend's home on Rosemont.

In contrast, the Higley family suffered the full wrath of the Pickens debris flow. Minutes before midnight, Lee Higley was in the dining room with his mother. Six-year-old Barbara was working a jigsaw puzzle (a popular pastime in those days). The father had gone outside once again to secure the sandbags. Lee remembers that at two minutes after twelve o'clock the lights went out. Suddenly, they heard the wall of destruction rumbling down on them. His mother had only time enough to scream, "Oh, it's too late!" Instantly, the house exploded, and all three were swept away. Lee remembers saving himself by clinging to a tree. Eventually, he was able to crawl through mud into his mother's car, where he honked the horn until rescuers arrived. Sister Barabara and her dog were found wandering down Rosemont Avenue. Later, brother and sister failed to recognize each other in their mud-drenched condition. They were taken to the single-engine fire station adjacent to St. Luke's, where they were provided with showers and cots to rest on. The next day, they were still washing the mud from their mouths.

Lee Higley, now a retired architect in his eighties, told me that he has never fully recovered from the trauma of losing both his parents that night. He and his sister became orphans in a matter of seconds. Homer Higley's body was found three days later in San Pedro Harbor. Ethel's remains were discovered soon after, close to the wreckage of her home.

From time to time, the forces of nature have unleashed some cruel weather-driven events. Our peaceful valley was on the receiving end of one of these assaults, and there are still survivors among us who carry the indelible scars in their memories. And yet, within this chaos and pain, we often find extraordinary acts of courage and selflessness. Marcie Warfield, an eleven-year-old girl, personified these traits. Six days after the flood, the *Los Angeles Times* featured a touching picture of her on its front page. She was in a hospital bed, a sad smile on her face, holding two brand-new dolls in her arms. The caption over her head read, "Child Heroine of Montrose Recovering. Girl Saves Unconscious Father and Brother."

Over the years, we often looked at the picture, wondering what ever became of that special girl. We had no clue as to her whereabouts or if she was alive and well. To our great surprise, Marcie Warfield Flannery phoned us one day on the seventy-sixth anniversary of the New Year's Flood. She invited us to her beach home in Oxnard. When we arrived in early January 2011, we were greeted by an agile lady in her late eighties. She had a personality that sparkled, coupled with a memory that bordered on total recall.

She related how her family came to rent a home at 2561 Mayfield, on the north side of the street, a stone's throw above the American Legion Hall. Her mother had passed away two years earlier, and her father, Charles, a car salesman, enlisted the aid of Mrs. Genevieve Wood, who came with "Little Edith," age six, to serve as housekeeper. Marcie had two brothers, Charles Jr. and Buddy, ages fourteen and six.

Marcie remembered that the family had a good Christmas, and now they were looking forward to New Year's morning. Their father had promised them a trip to the Pasadena Rose Parade. Two days prior to the great event, torrential rains intervened. On December 31, rocks and small boulders were bouncing down the streets. By early evening, Mayfield was blocked on both sides. Her dad was very concerned. The small wash on the east side of the house had become a raging cataract about to burst its banks. As the evening wore on, larger boulders began crashing against the back of the wood-frame home. Shortly before midnight, they gathered together in the front room while Mrs. Wood led them in the Lord's Prayer. Marcie said that she was about to "retrieve her mother's cameo and a small treasure chest in her bedroom when the building shook and the wall collapsed" as a fifteen-foot wave of mud and rock "knocked down the house, reducing it to kindling wood." All six were swept away. When she regained consciousness, she realized she was stripped of her clothing and covered with mud. She remembers extricating herself from the mire by "grabbing the tail of a large horse." Within minutes, two sturdy Civilian Conservation Corps workers arrived and carried her gently to the Legion Hall.

This is where a mystery unfolds. Did she experience two formidable debris flows that night? Marcie describes coming into the American Legion Hall covered in mud and seeing her father near the wall holding "Little Edith," and her six-

This view looking south from Mayfield toward Fairway shows dramatically how the ground was gouged out by the passage of massive boulders and rocks hurtling along at perhaps thirty miles per hour. It's amazing to consider that some people swept down these plunging rapids actually survived.

year-old brother, Buddy. As she approached them, she heard another deafening rumble as a massive debris flow tore a five- by ten-foot hole in the Legion Hall's northwest corner, flooding the interior quickly as refugees fought for their lives. The large piano slid across the room. The last words that she heard were an "adult" shouting, "Mayday! Mayday! Can you hear me?" According to her, all four were once more swept out into the horror of the storm. She survived by clinging to the railing on the front steps of the Legion Hall.

Were there two large, closely spaced debris flows that night, or is it possible that the deluge that actually destroyed the Warfield house came from the raging wash east of their property line? Whatever the case, this is Marcie's honest remembrance of a traumatic episode in her life that occurred almost eighty years ago.

None of this diminishes the act of a brave and resourceful young girl who, in spite of serious physical injuries, reached out to save her father and six-year-old brother from possible death as they struggled to survive in the heavy muck left in the wake of the debris flow. As Marcie remembered it:

> *After I was washed away from the Legion Hall's steps, I lost consciousness. When I awoke, I felt like I was encased in a cocoon of mud. I crawled to my feet in knee-deep mud, and didn't recognize anything in the semi darkness and rain. It looked like a moonscape. I heard moaning and crying in the distance. I cried out, "Is that you, Buddy?" Then my dad's voice came through weakly, "Marcie, is that you?" I said, "Keep talking Daddy." I dug out Buddy who was buried up to his neck. I found my dad hanging on to a telephone pole. I discovered a little coupe half buried, and scraped the mud from the windows and door handles. Somehow I was able to drag my six foot, 185 pound father and little brother into the car. The three of us huddled together for warmth. Later, I cleaned the headlights, blinking them on and off while honking the horn until three men arrived at dawn. Two of them helped my father. The third carried Buddy. I was able to walk to the waiting ambulance even though I had a broken ankle and punctured leg. Weeks later we learned that Charles Jr. was rescued after the house collapsed. Poor Mrs. Wood and "Little Edith" perished. We were all taken to separate hospitals and reunited several weeks later. When I talk about it, it's like telling the story about another little girl.*

Marcie was in a wheelchair for a while, under the care of an aunt. It seems she also had a skull fracture and a fractured hip. Buddy had a broken arm. The father's hip never healed properly. He limped the rest of his life.

This is the "exit wound" on the front side of the American Legion Hall. Of the thirty-some people inside the hall, some were shot out the front window and door (like little Marcie Warfield), while others took a more circuitous route down through a large section of the floor that gave way into the basement and then out through the basement wall. It's no wonder that so many died.

After the flood, Marcie never returned to the Crescenta Valley. She seldom talked about it. She didn't tell her late husband, Mike Flannery, about it until 1984, after she was interviewed by John Marshall on Channel 4 commemorating the fiftieth anniversary of the Crescenta Valley Flood that year. She always wanted to return to the valley someday and touch the hands of the survivors who shared her sad memories.

Her wish was fulfilled in May 2011, when she met a number of her fellow survivors at a special program held in the Community Room of our new La Crescenta Library. Marcie Warfield Flannery was warmly greeted as our "rediscovered survivor."

To the best of our knowledge, Marcie is the only living witness who was in the Legion Hall when the full force of the Pickens Canyon debris flow passed through. Mrs. Thomas Bonetto wrote a *Ledger* article describing the destruction of the Legion Hall based on volunteers who barely escaped. Although a member of the Red Cross Auxiliary, she was excused from duty that night by Myrtle Adams. These are some extracts from the *Ledger*:

Numerous calls for aid were received and Legionnaires responded, assisting many families. Coffee and hot toasted sandwiches were sent to those who were working to curb the raging waters. When the seriousness of the flood was realized, the Legion Hall was filled with homeless families. First aid was given when necessary. Mrs. Adams was assisted by Mrs. Vera Kahn, who had charge of the food supplies. Charles Poole was at the telephone, receiving calls for assistance…Dry blankets were needed and volunteers left the hall to go to the Red Cross hut on Ocean View to get them. [Excessive flooding blocked their return.]… *The refugees, about ten in number, were resting on cots or huddled about the furnace…Tob Lamar, commander of the post and Legionnaire, W. Passell, had just returned to the hall after assisting people caught in the torrents…Suddenly a loud roar was heard. Mr. Lamar and Mr. Passell ran for the door to see what had happened. Mrs. Adams, leaning against a door, her head raised toward heaven, was praying for the protection of God. Charles Poole was still at this post. The refugees still huddled by the fire. Crash! It had come. The surging waters were upon them. The northwest portion of the hall fell with the onslaught. Lamar and Passell were miraculously saved.* [Both leaped from the front porch into a small sycamore tree on the east side of the Legion Hall. It still stands, tall and stately, seventy-eight years later.] *Since Mr. Poole was in charge of the telephone that night, Marcie probably heard his "Mayday" cry before being washed out the front door. He remembered "seeing the piano tip backwards and then start sliding toward the door." He was making his way toward Mrs. Adams when he was "caught by a wall of water that tumbled and rolled him about until he reached Montrose Avenue" where he caught onto a bush. He was mired in silt up to his armpits. His mouth was filled with gravel, making it impossible to cry out for help. He gradually made his way to a stump in the middle of the street and waited there until three young men from a stalled car came to his rescue. An ambulance took him to a Pasadena hospital with an injured back, broken ribs, and serious eye infection. It took him three days to free his mouth of gravel. He remained there for six weeks. Ben Lenz, of the Montrose Radio Shop, personally installed a radio in his hospital room for the duration of his stay.*

Twelve good people were unable to escape the avalanche that savaged the interior of the Legion Hall that night. It turned out that the Gibraltar of the Valley was unable to ward off the full strength of Nature's wrath.

Among those unfortunate were Myrtle Adams and Vera De Woody Kahn, key volunteer Red Cross leaders who were always there to serve the needy in times of crisis. Five months after the tragedy, friends and neighbors gathered in the Memorial Grove at Clark Junior High School to plant a flowering eucalyptus tree honoring the memory of these valiant women.

After pillaging the Legion Hall, the unstoppable mass continued to spread east and west as it roared across Montrose Avenue. The McFarland home near the northwest corner of Rosemont and Montrose was overwhelmed by a ten-foot flood of debris. It filled every room in the house. The five celebrants, hosts and guests alike, spent hours that night standing on tables and windowsills. But they all lived to greet the dawn. The McFarland home at 2613 Montrose Avenue, built with solid stones and concrete, proved indeed to be their "Rock of Gibraltar." The Seventh-Day Adventist Church across the street on the southwest corner was destroyed. A year later, a new church emerged a quarter of a mile west on higher ground.

After surging across Montrose Avenue, this incredible force of destruction did not relent until it emptied into a raging river once known as Verdugo Creek.

A block below Montrose Avenue and one hundred yards or so west of Rosemont Avenue, Mr. and Mrs. Henry Hesse were hosting a New Year's party at 2631 Manhattan Avenue. Attending were twin brothers Winston and Weston Doty, popular cheerleaders at the University of Southern California, and their dates, Gladys Fisher and Mary Janet Cox. A family friend, Clark Harmon, rounded out the guest list. The chief conversation topics focused on the incessant rain and, naturally, the next day's Rose Bowl game, pitting powerful Stanford against the underdog, Columbia University.

At midnight, the twins called their mother and wished her a happy New Year. It was the last time she would hear their voices. Minutes later, Henry Hesse and his guests heard the deafening cacophony of the debris mass as it descended on the house. He glanced out the rear door in time to see the back porch disappear. Instinctively, he reached for his wife and ran to another escape route, shouting, "Everybody out!" They all rushed out into the swirling waters as the house began to crumble. Henry was able to put his wife astride a floating tree trunk. Both held on as it carried them for three blocks before it lodged against a concrete wall. They waited for the water to subside and then worked their way to safe ground. He told the rescue team that he "was confident that none of his guests survived." He was heart-breakingly correct. Today, there is no house or street number where the Hesse home once stood—only the wide Pickens Canyon Flood Channel confronts the eye. Four neighbors on both sides of the Hesse

These houses along Montrose Avenue to the west of Rosemont are buried in mud nearly up to the eaves. Many of these houses were dug out and repaired and are still there today, although one by one they are being replaced with apartments.

The next victim of the Pickens Canyon flow was the Seventh-Day Adventist church on the corner of Rosemont and Pickens Avenue, just below Montrose Avenue. It was fortunately unoccupied. *Courtesy of Joe and Linda Rakasits.*

Continuing south, the Pickens Canyon flow plowed through houses on Manhattan, Piedmont, Pleasure Way and Hermosa. The center of the channel is about where the Hesse house stood. The concrete Pickens Canyon Flood Control Channel follows this same route today.

family also lost their homes. Mrs. Etta Thomas's body was washed three miles into Glendale after her home at 2621 Manhattan collapsed.

Piedmont Avenue, a short block below Manhattan, harbors its own sad tales. One such tale involved Philip and Ruth Reihl, who lived on this street. Both had acquitted themselves with valor by helping to save the Ashrama during the November Pickens Fire that preceded the New Year's Flood. Philip, in particular, had been right on the frontlines with the firemen battling the flames. According to Philip, "Their thirteen years of companionship was wiped out in two minutes" when the rock-laden flood crashed through the front room. At 12:10 a.m., they wished each other "Happy New Year," and at 12:12 a.m., they were both swept away by the torrent. Ruth did not survive. Philip was washed two blocks onto the porch of a house. When they rescued him, he was covered beyond recognition in mud. From there, he was taken to a relief station in Montrose. He was badly bruised and in deep grief at the loss of his wife. He desperately sought the solace and refuge of the Ashrama. The Swamiji heard of his plight on New Year's Day and led a hazardous auto trip over rock-strewn roads to return Philip to his beloved Ashrama.

New Year's Day 1934

At the behest of the editor of the *Crescenta Valley Ledger*, S.S. "Scoop" Harralson of 2624 Piedmont Avenue was asked to write his eyewitness account of what he saw and heard shortly after 12:00 a.m. on January 1, 1934. It is perhaps the best description of what happens when a swift-moving mass of rock, water and debris plows through an unsuspecting neighborhood in the middle of the night:

> *The jazz and whoopee of midnight celebrations blasting from radios all up and down the 2600 block on Piedmont Avenue.*
>
> *Lights shone from almost all the windows except the bedrooms where the children were sleeping—and there were 21 children in that block.*
>
> *It was raining, had been all day, and the little wash across Piedmont Avenue and Rosemont was bank-full and growling at the overload of mud and stones.*
>
> *And then—there came a sound that over-toned the noise of the rain and the growl of the wash and the blasting of the radios. A rumble, a dull roar, the walls shook, the lights flickered.*
>
> *Curiosity, rather than fear, sent my wife and me to the front porch, and right then everything changed. Sounds changed and the night became hideous with noise.*
>
> *Sounds of breaking timbers as homes were smashed, hoarse shouts of men, screams of women and children and that sullen rumble of tons of stone as they were carried by on an avalanche of mud.*
>
> *One moment the home of the McDonalds' glowed with light and as we watched we saw the wall of mud and stones and water and debris that was carried on its crest. From six to seven feet high the wall came on and the next moment there was nothing left to show where the home had been.*
>
> *From the north, electric light wires flashed like nitrogen flares, where they burned in half in a hundred places, and then—darkness. And still the noise of cracking timbers as the water crossed the road and other homes passed out of the picture—and still the cries and screams of and groans of the families washed away—and still the roar and rumble of the mud flood.*
>
> *As the impending doom swept toward us at racetrack speed, my wife said, "This about ends it all, we're through"—but she stayed on the porch. I remember telling her that if it was the end, we'd take it on the chin, facing it. But something happened. The wall seemed to dip on our side. On to the porch came mud and stones—stones weighing from 50 to 500 pounds—the floor was covered—but still we stood as the water and sticks and small stones and mud flowed into the front room to a depth of*

four inches—and not a stone had landed against our legs or feet. Funny, isn't it?

In two minutes the deluge was past, grinding and tumbling and screaming on its way to the river, carrying with it death and destruction, and still we stood on the porch unscratched, but in mud to our knees.

Was it over? Was there more coming? What had happened? What to do? What should we do? How could we help? Whom should we help? The answer came from the top of a pile of debris which morning showed to be three automobiles in the yard. A hand and arm showed, and a strangled cry for help—a wade through waist-deep muck and I found myself helping a large woman out of the wreckage and into the house. For the next 15 minutes hysterical screams were all of the response we could get to our excited questions. She had seen her family and relatives and friends carried into the dark—she had held onto the hand of her blind father until the pull of the mud had taken him from her—she had seen her sister-in-law and two months old baby blotted out of sight—she had lost her husband. My wife finally quieted her and gave her some warm dry clothing and then we all three waded across and down the street to the home of J.W. Lawyer, which stood on higher ground and which had not been touched. There we found another story. A young woman, covered with mud and thoroughly soaked, had just been brought into the house after having been swept three blocks downstream from the American Legion Hall. She was dazed but apparently unhurt. A few minor scratches and bruises were the sum total of her injuries.

An hour later she related what had happened up to the time—when she was washed overboard from the Legion Hall. I did not learn her name.
[This young girl must have been Marcie Warfield.]

Repeated trips from the house over all portions of the few streets where walking was possible brought no further results. Nothing could be done in the dark and it was still raining—two roaring streams of water were barriers to any exit for a space three blocks long and one block wide. We were entirely isolated—no lights—no water—no telephones, and no one with the slightest idea of what it was all about, what had really happened, nor the extent of the loss of life. No one slept—no one was sleepy—no one thought of eating—a cup of coffee might have helped, but there was no water. I thought that it must be near dawn after the hours and hours that had passed. I looked at the clock. It was 2:15 a.m.

Our son, Ernest, was attending a New Year's in the 2800 block on Montrose Avenue. What had happened there? Was he safe and would he stay that way? Suspense was nerve-wracking as the minutes dragged on like hours.

Three-thirty and a hello came from the house that we had deserted. It was the boy. He had swam and waded and been rolled down both streams across the road as he fought his way home. He had been carried two blocks below the house. He was bruised and bloody, but still smiling. From him we got the news that our home was the only one standing for two blocks. That told us many things.

Morning came with a drizzle, and we could see where the other homes in the back had been, but there was nothing left to even offer a suggestion of where the foundations had once been. Gone completely and entirely. Where?

Mud, mud, mud, and more mud. The homes of Grayber, Wilson, and Correa on our side of the street had gone down with the torrent, and only the debris and a few oak trees showed above the 3 foot mud floor. The entire landscape had been changed in just a few minutes and the death angel had spread his wings for blocks around, taking the young and the aged and the weak. Men hovered about the wreckage which marked the spots where their homes had been, searching for one or many missing loved ones. Heart-broken screams from husband or father announced the finding of mud soaked broken bodies, and another gruesome job for stretcher bearers. Hour after hour throughout the day of January first, six men with blanket covered burdens tramped slowly from the destroyed section to the improvised morgue in the center of Montrose. Eyes grew tired and hearts grew sick watching the silent parade.

Another son was absent from our home, Wayne, and nothing had been heard from him. He might have accepted a New Year's dinner invitation from friends in San Bernardino. He might have been in Los Angeles. He might—but what was the use? And then at 6 o'clock he came, unharmed, unhurt, but badly scared, for he had learned less than an hour before about the disaster.

Daylight had shown what had happened so near our home. In our yard, on past the house in the rear, are two pianos, a couple of trunks, a cement manhole casing and cover, broken furniture, and at least a dozen boulders weighing not less than five tons. These had all been swept down the driveway to be deposited in the rear. In the front yard were three automobiles, a chest of silver in a trunk, a radio, the side of a house, and rocks and mud. The entire place is covered with small light articles, and more are buried underneath the muck which is rapidly hardening. The first day we dug up a rabbit, a chicken, a goat, and in a pool of dirty water we found two goldfish, alive and well, apparently.

This sturdy stone house stood firm and strong against the impact of the flood but was gutted. Doors, windows and everything inside the house are gone.

The Pickens Canyon flow continued to dig a deep channel until it reached Honolulu, where it flattened out somewhat. Even though most of the large rocks had dropped out of the debris flow by that point, the mud continued on, causing devastation on Sycamore and La Crescenta Avenue below Honolulu.

Mr. Harralson's compassion for the children must have centered on the Wilson family, who lost three offspring when their home was washed away at 2636 Piedmont that night. Sam, ten; Homer, eight; and Betty, two, all fell victim to a force beyond their comprehension. Marddie Marie Wilson, fourteen, died almost a year later from injuries sustained in the flood. She left behind heart-broken parents and a brother, Ollan Wilson.

A total of six homes were destroyed and five damaged on the 2600 block. The Harralson place was not severely damaged, and more importantly, their two boys returned safely to their parents, albeit bruised and exhausted.

The mayhem continued as the convulsive debris flow, nearly a block wide, smashed across Hermosa, Honolulu and Sycamore Avenues. One house was destroyed and two washed away on Hermosa. Five suffered the same fate on Honolulu. Poor Mrs. Eugena Scully's stone bastion failed to save her from the onslaught. Miraculously, her four daughters found safety by climbing into the sturdy oak tree in the family's garden. A neighbor rescued them several hours later.

Sycamore Avenue was the last to be lambasted by the cataclysm before it plunged into the Verdugo Wash. Seven more homes were leveled or washed away on this street.

Pleasure Way, a short north–south thoroughfare extending from Piedmont to Honolulu, had only three homes, all on its east side. These structures were completely obliterated by the ferocity of the flood. In the following days, even the local postman had difficulty pointing to their former locations. The Correa family, at 3934 Pleasure Way, lost their seventeen-year-old son, Joseph, when he was swept away in the wreckage of the house. He became one of several bodies recovered in San Pedro Harbor, forty miles away from their loved ones. Thankfully, this concludes the tragic drama of the Pickens Canyon rampage.

GOSS/EAGLE/SHIELDS CANYONS

The last powerful debris flow to be discussed caused serious damage but thankfully took no lives. This flow was unique in that it was formed from water and debris originating in three separate canyons. The mouths of these canyons are within a quarter of a mile of one another. From east to west, Goss emerges a mile above Foothill at the top of Rosemont, Eagle enters from a mountain slope east of the Pine Crest housing tract and Shields empties at the very top of Pine Cone Road. The three merge a mile below where El Caminito Street intersects with La Crescenta Avenue. The combined flows continued southwest for almost a mile over sparsely settled land. The destruction commenced beyond Foothill, when the flood of water, boulders, rocks and mud surged through the intersection of Ramsdell and Community Avenues and down onto Prospect, an east–west street, where Charles and Hazel Crowe lived with their three young boys, Kirk, Victor and Bobby. A graphic account of what they all experienced that night was included in a letter that Charles wrote to his mother and sister in Iowa several days after the disaster. Fortunately, the letter was preserved.

It is a remarkable story of one man's determination to protect his family and elderly neighbors from a merciless debris flow that threatened to turn their home into a death trap.

On December 31, from 2:00 p.m. on, the never-ending rain intensified. That evening, an elderly couple sought refuge with the Crowes. The wife required a wheelchair. Later, a lady about eighty years old asked for protection. To make additional room, Charles asked Victor and Kirk to stay overnight with the young couple next door. They were more than happy to oblige. No one felt like celebrating, and so they all turned in early. As Charles tells it:

> It was just 12 midnight…when Hazel and I bounced out of bed when we were awakened by a terrific roaring, like continuous thunder. As I hit the floor, my feet struck ice cold water and mud. I looked in towards the front room when a great wall of water, boulders, rock and sand struck the front of the house, tearing the front door off…and in just a second we were above our knees in water and sand. We could hardly hear each other shout…I was terrified but tried to keep my head. The first thing I thought of was to let the torrent out through the double French doors at the back of the house. [Shades of Harold Nuzum on Encinal Avenue.] I had a terrific battle against the current, but finally opened them wide, and pulled the dining room table between them to keep them open as the swirling black mass rushed out…I heard Bobby cry out and I waded back into the bedroom where he had fallen out into the swirling waters. I picked him out and tossed him onto the bed. Skippy, the dog, bounded in and onto the bed with him.

Charles then quickly boosted wife Hazel up into the attic access opening inside their clothes closet. Bobby and his dog made the next ascent. Never flagging, Charles carried the eighty-year-old woman through the muck up to where Hazel could reach out and assist. He and the husband then carried and pushed the crippled wife into the attic along with her parrot and cat. They salvaged as much dry clothing and bedding as they could find and passed it up to the shivering survivors. Somehow, Charles was also able to cram two mattresses through the hole. He wrote, "All this time the water was rising, and as I watched the black stuff creeping up, I began to wonder what my experience was going to be like while drowning in that thick stuff. I didn't think that we had a ghost of a chance, and fully expected to be destroyed, but knew I must keep taking advantage of every little thing I could think of." Finally, they were all bedded down in the attic, above a not-too-stable foundation, while rocks and boulders assaulted the exterior walls.

When the waters started to recede, he slogged over to the young couple's place, apprehensive about his boys. He waded into the front room hip high in mud, calling plaintively for Kirk and Victor, to no avail. Charles explained his sense of hopelessness: "I felt sure they had been washed away. I went into the bedroom and flashed my light. The beds were floating, but no life. I called once more in desperation, and like music from the heavens, a voice answered. The two boys, and the young couple, were huddled up in a four-foot attic. They were trembling in their cold wet pajamas. Mr. Crowe carried the boys, one at a time, to the arms of their loving mother. The young couple came too." Charles wrote the following about their sleeping arrangement: "We all spent the rest of the night in the attic. Ten people, three puppies and their bulldog mother, our dog Skippy, a parrot, a cat and our two love birds." Somehow, the lovebirds were unscathed, having survived in their cage amid a bombardment of rocks and rubble.

Days later, Charles was still dealing with cuts on the bottoms of his feet. He and Hazel also suffered from what he called "mud-poisoning" on their lower legs. Charles surmised that "poison oak, sumac and other poisonous grasses" had mixed with the mud from the burned-over mountain slopes.

I have included only a portion of Charles Crowe's letter here. The entire letter is a good read and is included in its entirety in the "Flood Stories and Eyewitness Accounts" section.

He signed his letter to his mother and sister, "With Love and Best Wishes, Charlie, Letter Carrier 47, Glendale, Calif." Charles Crowe was much more than "Letter Carrier 47." His service to family and neighbors in crisis is a testimony to the "goodness of the human spirit."

Goss, Eagle and Shields Canyons combined to send a debris flow roaring through well-populated neighborhoods below Foothill between Pennsylvania and Ramsdell Avenues. *Courtesy of Joe and Linda Rakasits.*

Valley pioneer Chuck Bausback lived with his parents on Evelyn Street a block below Prospect. Six years before his passing, he typed a brief remembrance of what occurred in his home during the tense hours preceding the midnight cloudburst and violent canyon discharges that followed. He was only eleven at the time, but his recollections were both vivid and precise. Early in the evening, they decided to do jigsaw puzzles, a big fad in those days. It was a way of passing time prior to greeting the New Year. It also kept their minds off the constant rain beating against the house. The once small creek west of the property was bursting its banks. The destruction of the small bridge across the wash intensified their fears. When his dad called the emergency center for more sand bags, the answer was: "Sir, at this point we are only trying to save lives!" And "then, nine minutes after midnight our house shook so violently that many of my jigsaw pieces fell to the floor. We thought that it was an earthquake! We did not realize how lucky we were!" The next morning, their yard on the west side was piled high with boulders and wreckage. Across the wash, their neighbor's home had been cut in half. Six hours earlier, the heavy torrent of debris- and boulder-laden water had missed their house completely

They still faced challenges. There was no electricity, gas or drinking water. Fortunately, his mother always kept an emergency supply of food and bottles of water on hand. Mom's precautions saved the day since they were also marooned between two turbulent streams, moving rapidly from the mountains. The map shows a segment of the Shields Canyon flow breaking away high above Foothill. The Bausbacks were marooned between these two streams for a number of days. Fear not, they had a small battery-powered radio, allowing them to keep in touch with the outside world. Two days later, it was frustrating to hear the Red Cross broadcast that they were numbered among the dead. After eleven days of isolation, the truck arrived in their area with potable water. They crossed the still rushing creek, on planks, to fill their water containers. Chuck was the first to inform the truck driver that the family's drowning had been "greatly exaggerated." The truck driver was shocked and insisted that at least one of the family members drive with him to Red Cross headquarters and correct the misinformation. Naturally, the eleven-year-old volunteered. No doubt, Chuck was the star of the show when he informed them that they were all still alive!

Chuck closed his remembrance on a slight note of humor:

> *I was in Montrose on the day that the Los Angeles Sheriff arrived in his big Cadillac followed by a squadron of motorcycle policemen in order to inspect the flood damage first hand. He got out of his car, resplendent in his uniform, and fell into a sinkhole filled with quicksand, where he sank to his armpits! His squadron had to find a rope to throw, and some planks to lay on the quicksand, so they could reach him and pull him out. As soon as he was out, he jumped into his Cadillac, told his chauffer to head to Los Angeles, and was never heard from again.*

This sheriff was very popular. I hesitate to use his name.

Three blocks below the Bausback home on Evelyn Street, Mr. and Mrs. Carl Gee had a chicken ranch at 3113 Mayfield Avenue. Mr. Gee had a big day ahead of him and chose to turn in early. The local paper played up the story that his wife cajoled him into getting dressed in case the heavy rains posed a hazard to life and property.

Once again, in a matter of seconds, a hardworking husband and wife lost their home and livelihood. The swath of mud and rubble still had enough energy to sweep their dwelling three hundred feet across the street into a large tree. Most of the chickens were gone. The equipment was ruined. What they missed most were the family pictures and silverware. With all of their loss, their morale was high because they knew they had each other.

The inky mass continued its downward journey—rolling over Honolulu and damaging nine more homes on west Sycamore before joining the muddy waters of Verdugo Creek.

DUNSMORE CANYON

On the evening of December 31, high in the northwest corner of the valley, the Swamiji and his followers at the Ashrama were fighting valiantly to save their cherished retreat from the protracted rainstorm. Relying on flashlights to see, they worked desperately to divert the canyon flows from their sacred temple and other buildings. The temple patio had become a small lake, and a waterfall was flowing down the steps of Temple Hill. Then suddenly, at midnight, they heard a deafening roar, making it impossible to hear one another's shouts. A cloudburst had taken place, releasing countless tons of pent-up mountain debris. At a higher level, some saw what appeared to be a series of lightning strikes, but they proved to be dozens of high-tension lines that had gone down, setting off dramatic flashes across the sky. The roar was an enormous flash flood bursting from the innards of Dunsmore Canyon onto the top of New York Avenue.

After the flooding lessened, the Swamiji and faithful Brother George made an inspection tour westward toward Dunsmore Canyon. With great caution, the two men picked their way over shattered electrical poles and fallen wires. They were stunned to discover a one-hundred-foot gap between the Ashrama and the Le Mesnager properties. Water was still roaring and raging southward, with large boulders bouncing along with the turbulence. A day after this, photographs were taken of two huge boulders sitting in the middle of New York Avenue brought down by this furious torrent. Witnesses said that the boulders literally danced on the paved road along with the floodwaters, rocks and uprooted trees. Each one weighed over sixty tons! Swamiji and George were appalled and saddened to see that the small brown cottage at the top of New York had vanished. Only a small portion of the chimney remained. It had once been the secluded domicile of Dr. McIntyre, his wife and small baby. (The family evacuated prior to the disaster.)

With the exception of the McIntyre home, the *Ledger* survey does not list any other home that was destroyed on New York Avenue. There was evidently enough open space in the early '30s to allow such a flow to spread harmlessly and dissipate as Nature intended.

Luckily, no such deluge had an impact on the Ashrama. This is not to suggest that the Ashrama survived untouched. A car parked near Temple Hill slid into a deep ditch, and a mudslide threatened its library. A gaping hole was discovered below the parking lot—fifteen feet deep and fifteen feet wide—stretching some distance into the orchard.

New Year's Day 1934

This photo is taken from the San Gabriel Mountains looking down at the Le Mesnager vineyards. The roofless burned stone barn is in the center, surrounded by charred and flooded grapevines. The Dunsmore Canyon flow can be seen spreading out through the sagebrush and vineyards below. The area shown in this photo is now Deukmejian Wilderness Park.

Just below the mouth of Dunsmore Canyon, at the top of New York Avenue, these massive boulders were deposited in the middle of the road, testifying to the incredible power of the Dunsmore Canyon flow. The boulders made for some interesting photo opportunities as cars parked next to them were dwarfed by their shear size.

The big problem centered on the lack of running water for human needs. "The big lead pipes which brought their drinking water...were twisted, broken and shattered." Thanks to the ingenuity of Brother George, they were able to tap a small stream to sustain the community until repairs could be made.

Meanwhile, with tractor, truck and energetic manpower, they filled in the holes and the eroded gullies. But they felt frustrated because their forced isolation prevented them from doing active relief work among their brethren one mile below.

Within a few days of the tragedy, a service was conducted for Ruth Reihl followed by cremation. At a later date, a service was held at the beach where her ashes joined the vast Pacific Ocean.

It was not long before they could say, "The Ashrama stands and shines in the beautiful sunshine during the daytime and like a beautiful maiden in the moonlight, as if nothing had happened." In God's good time, Philip Reihl rallied, surprising everyone with his happy nature once again. Although lame and bruised, he continued to labor for the Ashrama. Some time ago, I came across a *Ledger* article dated February 10, 1963. The lead caption read, "Longtime Resident Retires to Old Soldiers Home." Beneath it was a picture of "Sgt. Philip Leopold Reihl." He had lived at the Ashrama, "a safe retreat in the wilderness above La Crescenta," since his wife perished in the "Great La Crescenta Flood of 1934." His stay there had only been broken by a two-year study of Yoga in India. His next address would be the Old Soldiers' Home in West Los Angeles. The article closed with these words: "Like another famous General, Philip will tell you that 'Old soldiers never die. They just fade away.' Sergeant Reihl expects to do just that at the Old Soldiers Home." He was seventy-eight at the time of this interview.

Cooks Canyon

Traveling westward, Santa Carlotta Avenue passes the mouth of Cooks Canyon, just a few hundred yards beyond Boston Avenue. There is a substantial dip in the road at this point. Viewed from above, Cooks Canyon resembles a deep-cut, rocky riverbed with steep walls as high as sixty feet. Today, one can see several homes that appear to be precariously perched near the edge. In the '30s, there was ample open country below to safely accommodate the debris flows of yesteryear. It was part of a natural process.

Pioneer resident Barbara Johnson lived in the Highway Highlands tract, between Dunsmore and Boston, below Foothill. After the 1934 flood, she recalls that the grape vineyards above Foothill caught all of the debris. In Barbara's own words, "We got only water. Our streets had been paved the year before the flood so they carried the water away beautifully." That is the way nature used to work prior to the heavy population growth along the alluvial fan below the south face of the San Gabriels.

This story is a fitting way to round out the human drama, both poignant and inspiring, that characterized so much of that tumultuous New Year's morning. The Lorenz family risked their lives on two occasions in the Crescenta Valley. They literally braved fire and flood before they became permanent residents once again. As previously mentioned, Bob Lorenz and his family were forced to evacuate their home in Briggs Terrace when the Pickens Fire swept through at two o'clock in the morning. They lost their home and possessions and were forced to share a home with the grandparents "down the hill" in Los Angeles.

They sorely missed their friends in the Foothills and decided to make a visit after Christmas. Despite the heavy rain, the family caravanned in two cars up the hill on New Year's Eve. As Mike Lawler wrote in his weekly column for the *Crescenta Valley Weekly* newspaper, "Unbeknownst to them, they were headed into a disaster zone." They had a warm evening with their friends who lived off Briggs Avenue above Foothill. "Just before midnight there was a massive cloudburst, and a few minutes later, as they toasted the New Year, the ground began to shake. They listened in terror as what sounded like a fast moving train roared past them. That was the sound of thousands of tons of boulders and logs headed down Pickens Canyon." That led to a quick goodbye.

In a matter of minutes, they were on their way down Briggs Avenue. When they reached Foothill, they found La Crescenta unrecognizable. Streets and buildings were gone. Boulders and mud made passage almost impossible. Somehow, the two cars got separated. The mother's car got mired in the mud, forcing them to spend a cold, damp night in the car. Bob, age eleven, was in his father's car, which bogged down in front of the Bluebird Diner while attempting to climb Pennsylvania Avenue. They were overjoyed to see the waiters waving them inside. Lawler writes that "Bob remembers one humorous incident from their night in the diner. In the wee hours of the morning, when nothing was moving, they spotted a big fancy sedan headed slowly down Pennsylvania Avenue. They rushed outside to flag them down, but as it rolled past them and disappeared into the dark, they could see there was no one in the car!" The Lorenz family survived their bout with Mother Nature for the second time and summarily rebuilt their home in Briggs Terrace. They earned their right to be permanent residents!

9

VOLUNTEERS AND GOVERNMENT WORKERS MEET THE CHALLENGES OF FLOOD DEVASTATION

This private party is all over, and from now on this building will be used as a hospital, if not a morgue!
—*Captain Blake*

The La Crescenta Woman's Club is located on the northeast corner of Piedmont and La Crescenta Avenues. The capricious flood left this community treasure unscathed. A Pasadena sorority, unaware of the tribulations beyond its walls, was enjoying a festive New Year's Eve party when a mud-soaked man and woman appeared at the entrance. After being told that it was a private party, the man, Captain Blake of the Forestry Service, informed the incredulous group, "This private party is all over, and from now on this building will be used as a hospital, if not a morgue!"

Soon thereafter, the first of the injured arrived. Nine more were helped inside for first aid. For two days, it did indeed resemble a crowded hospital. Later, the patients were transferred to a better staffed facility at the Sparr Heights Community Center located a mile south of Montrose. Eighteen doctors and forty nurses were on duty there. Red Cross personnel served at both locations.

Members of the Woman's Club worked in shifts around the clock for a week or more preparing a refuge for the homeless. The kitchen was always open for emergency workers and displaced residents. It was a godsend for the hundreds of laborers assigned to the flood-torn area by the Civil Works Administration. They fed four to five hundred emergency personnel each day.

Many refugees had lost their homes or were too weak to fend for themselves. Shoes and bedding were in great demand. There was always enough to go around. One of the more orderly volunteers complained, "The main room of the Clubhouse looked like a bargain basement after a hard day's bargain hunting." However, these women had every reason to be proud of themselves. Said one tired helper, "The La Crescenta Woman's Club has earned its niche in the Crescenta Valley Hall of Fame."

It had to be very difficult for most people in the valley as they faced the dawn of a new day and a new year only to confront a moonscape. The *Ledger* lists 158 damaged homes. A number of these damaged homes were effectively uninhabitable. Food and water were not readily available in the first hours. Some, like the Bausbacks, were marooned for a week or more. To ameliorate these needs, it took time and effort. Even the affluent Bissell family was trapped at their High Up Ranch, a mile above Foothill, when the bridge leading to their estate was washed out. Since they had no telephone service, eastern relatives were worried about them. A lone man on horseback had to "dig out and retreat" in his attempt to reach the ranch.

The Reverend Patrick Healy opened the Holy Redeemer Catholic Church to shelter the cold victims from the storm. The rumor mill reported parishioners finding a body in front of the church wall on their way to morning Mass. Rumors were rampant and seldom verified.

The Montrose Methodist and Seventh-Day Adventist Churches were destroyed. They continued to hold services in the Presbyterian sanctuary until they were able to relocate or rebuild.

It must have seemed incredulous to those still digging out of their misery to hear that the Pasadena Rose Parade was going on as usual. At least the planners inadvertently chose a fitting theme: "Tales of the Seven Seas." Noah was unavailable as grand marshal!

The scheduled Rose Bowl game was the second shocker. Remember, the stadium is barely five miles east of the Crescenta Valley. In 1934, it was the only bowl game in the nation. Pasadena's city fathers were determined that, "come hell or high water," our Stanford Indians, the coast's best team, were going to have an opportunity to roll over Columbia University's "paltry" Lions. Most fans perceived the Lions as lambs being led to the slaughter.

On the morning of January 1, the field looked like a small lake. The fire department was called to pump out the water. They did their best, but the surface was still soaked. Only thirty-five thousand could get there, the lowest number since its construction in 1922. Both teams slipped and splashed about for four quarters. To make a long game very short, the Columbia Lions triumphed over the Stanford Indians, 7–0.

Back in the devastated Crescenta Valley, water deliveries were a top priority. Emergency tank trucks were constantly on the move. The Civil Works Administration provided $10,000 in funds for water. One touching story involves Mrs. Jean Sharp of La Crescenta, who gave birth to a baby girl during the chaos. A forestry truck carried a tank of water to within a half mile of the Sharp home before bogging down. Fire wardens carried the water for the infant's bath in buckets the rest of the way. Donkeys and burros usually carried water over difficult terrain. Eventually, two thousand feet of two-and-a-half-inch hose was laid between central La Crescenta and western Montrose to serve as a temporary water supply for the town. Puritas Distilled Water Company donated a large tank to La Crescenta and provided a huge tank truck for the thirsty populace. By January 12, water was piped to the Crescenta Mutual Water Co. from the Valley Water Co. in La Canada. Clearly, there was resourceful leadership to tackle the multitude of problems left in the wake of the gigantic mountain debris flow.

The Salvation Army had a corps of fifteen workers at its Community House in Montrose. They provided hot meals and clothing for hundreds each day. Fifty Boy Scouts from the Verdugo Council, acting on orders from the local sheriff, assisted in cleanup and security. On any given day, one might see helpers from the La Cañada Thursday Club, Knights of Columbus, Salvation Army and the Mothers' Auxiliary of the Glendale Boy Scouts lending a hand to friends and neighbors.

The Civil Works Administration was one of the early New Deal programs sponsored by President Roosevelt. Rather than put the unemployed on the dole, he supported programs that put them to work at a sustaining wage. When possible, they hired the locals for their projects. Over 3,600 CWA workers were assigned to the Crescenta Valley area, including 110 trucks and drivers. They made rapid progress removing boulders and debris with tractors, scoopers, steam shovels and bulldozers. Thirty dump trucks hauled load after load of rocks and sediment, pouring it into huge holes and gullies created by the flood.

Much of the work required a pick and shovel. "One of the workers, a Negro, gets up every day at 3 a.m. to walk from Los Angeles to work for the CWA. Once in a while he is able to get a ride." The men often unearthed lost treasures swept away by the flood. These articles included kitchen utensils, sinks, bathtubs, radios, children's bicycles, scooters, typewriters, etc. On January 30, a silver pie server was found near Ocean View, stamped with the initials "V.D." It was certain that the server piece belonged to Mrs. Ward

Mail delivery was a problem after the flood as so many houses were vacated or destroyed. Here we see Montrose Letter Carrier No. 2 on his route making notes as to which addresses were still good. At the moment this photo was taken, he had already listed thirty-five addresses as entirely gone.

Community groups pulled together after the disaster to provide comfort to flood victims. At this relief center, the American Legion and a group of Boy Scouts are peeling potatoes to feed both victims and cleanup workers.

Power equipment cleared some roadways of mud. These two heavy vehicles are seen working on Honolulu Boulevard near the intersection with Orangedale. Just to the left is where Trader Joe's is located today.

Post-flood cleanup was often done by hand, as it was hard to get heavy equipment into the area. In this view looking south on Ocean View near Glenada, we see volunteers clearing the road of mud and rocks with shovels. Behind the workers is the mud-splattered but intact real estate office of Lillian Green, the "optimistic realtor."

Van Deusen, president of the La Crescenta Woman's Club. The server was a wedding gift that had been washed away with other belongings when the Van Deusen home on Castle Road was badly damaged in the storm. A Montrose man returned it to the grateful owner.

The Los Angeles County Flood Control, although spread thin throughout the district, offered both manpower and equipment. Its engineers provided invaluable assistance and direction to the outside organizations here for the emergency.

Governor Rolph also reached out to the flood-ravaged area. He ordered that all available Civil Works and other relief funds be made available to those in need. The Glendale mayor requested and received some heavy trucks to remove the debris from the streets.

From the onset, martial law was declared, and special permits were required to enter the flood-stricken valley. This did not deter the souvenir hunters, "who parked beyond the barricades and walked in to loot the damaged homes." One hundred deputies were put on duty to keep the "bothersome jackals" away from private property. It had been reported to Sheriff Biscailuz that looters were actually removing plumbing fixtures and built-in cabinets from damaged structures. He was determined to bring them to justice!

New Year's Day 1934

The morning after the flood, it was bright and sunny. This homeowner has pulled all the sodden items out of his house to dry in the sun. With many "lookie-loos" streaming to the valley, looting was a problem. Unattended items like this were tempting to sightseers, and some returning flood victims found people in their damaged homes going through their personal items. *Courtesy of Fern Stewart Hoag.*

Eleven-year-old Chuck Bausback heard his elementary teacher tell that when she returned to her home two days after New Year's Eve, she found the front of her home gone and heard female voices in her bedroom haggling over the clothes in her closet. (We have no record of how she responded to this "home invasion.") Many property owners had to literally "sit on their possessions." "Washings on the clotheslines are not safe," said one housewife.

Residents were not happy three weeks into January when the devastated area was opened to the public. They resented their morbid curiosity and the questions that came with it. A reporter wrote that the guards at the entrances to these streets embellished the truth by greatly exaggerating the actual death toll: "Oh yes, they take bodies out every day, but they won't tell where they get them or what is done with them."

The Red Cross came up with a clever but legal plan to partially lessen the annoyance of what the *Ledger* described as "the ever-present thousands of sightseers who, down through the ages, have flocked to the scene of every great disaster!" (In present-day parlance, we call them "lookie-loos.") The plan was simple and compassionate. The Red Cross stationed pretty girls from the American Legion Auxiliary on each corner

Dead flood victims were difficult to locate, often coming to rest under wrecked buildings or snagged in the roots of trees and buried under several feet of mud and rocks. Here, workers search for the dead, while a ghoulish group of sightseers looks on. *Courtesy of Joe and Linda Rakasits.*

in the valley on Saturday afternoons and all day on Sunday. With tin cup in hand, the girls asked the occupants in each car to contribute to the flood relief fund. At the close of the weekend, it was determined that this was the first proven instance that "any good" had ever come from the likes of such a curious crowd. The Red Cross was startled and gratified to learn that the donations totaled $1,233. This was a tidy sum to receive in the depth of the Great Depression.

Among the illustrious visitors was Governor James Rolph Jr. ("Sunny Jim"), who opted for an auto tour of the devastation. His official car became mired in the mud and had to be towed out, much to the amusement of the laborers. On January 5, the *Ledger* poked fun at him for his standoffishness: "He was always surrounded by a multitudinous number of deputy sheriffs. None of us could shake his hand." (So much for politics!)

A phenomenal and joyful ceremony was held in La Crescenta on July 7, 1934, six months and seven days after the New Year's Day tragedy. Ground was broken for the new home of Verdugo Hills American Legion Post 288. The new site was a gift from Mr. and Mrs. Thomas Bonetto Sr. It was located on La Crescenta Avenue directly across the street from the La Crescenta Woman's Club, which was untouched by the flood.

Amazingly, on August 29, 1934, they moved the former Legion Hall from its original foundations, one-half mile west, to the new site where remodeling

New Year's Day 1934

Someone has propped up the sign from Johnston's Garage next to the overturned tow truck from Johnston's Garage.

California governor James "Sunny Jim" Rolph toured the disaster area soon after the flood. He and his entourage stand outside the American Legion Hall surveying the incredible damage. *Courtesy of Joe and Linda Rakasits.*

added twelve feet to the front of the old building. A spacious lower room with kitchens was added for the women's auxiliary and the Boy Scout troop, which held meetings there. It has become a favorite choice for civic and social events, including wedding receptions. Bless the veterans of the Great War (World War I), who worked under the supervision of Tob Lamar, commander of Post 288, on their own time without pay to resurrect the old fortress. Also, bless those veterans of yesteryear who saw fit to honor the ultimate sacrifice of Myrtle Adams and Vera De Woody Kahn by making it the "memorial" hall. This honored all of the women who served in the Legion's Red Cross Auxiliary over the decade.

10

FLOOD CONTROL—A PLEA FOR HELP

I looked out the attic window and into the torrent. A woman screamed and yelled for help as she was sweeping by. She disappeared in a second.
—Charles Crowe

The citizens of the Crescenta Valley responded mightily to the two calamities spaced six weeks apart. It reflected their resiliency in times of distress, yet the stress factor would be there for months to come. In 1934, federal aid was not automatically forthcoming in the wake of a major disaster, natural or otherwise. The primary concern was the threat of future flooding. Rains in late October caused minor damage but alarmed everyone. The *Ledger* wrote sarcastically, "The smaller loss is not due to protective works inspired by the grim lesson of last January, but solely to the fact that the storm was only a quarter as severe as its predecessor." The paper rejected the excuse that the County Flood Control District had no money. The truth was that they had been lacking in funding since the 1926 bond issue was turned down. A desperate board of supervisors placed another bond issue on the ballot after the flood to cover improvements in the foothills, including the construction of debris basins and cement flood channels. It was rejected by a 4 percent margin.

Financial leaders in the valley, working with the board of supervisors, had some success negotiating for federal loans from the Reconstruction Finance Corporation, but the process was very slow at first. The Reconstruction

Finance Corporation was actually started by President Hoover to stem the tide of the Depression. It loaned millions of dollars to banks, railroads and businesses. It later became the key financial agency of Roosevelt's New Deal. The program, which continued until 1942, had a high percentage of ultimate repayment.

On January 4, 1935, Grace Carpenter, owner and editor of the *Ledger*, sent a memorable "open" letter to the first lady, Eleanor Roosevelt, with a petition signed by one thousand children. It was a personal plea, asking the first lady to cut through the red tape of the Reconstruction Finance Corporation and grant an "unconditional loan" for the construction of a permanent flood relief system in the valley. She asked Eleanor to remember, "You are our universal mother." A month later, the county board received a $4,132,000 check, $1,000,000 of which was earmarked for the valley. It was not nearly enough, but it surely helped.

Although the New Year's Day Flood of 1934 was mostly confined to the Crescenta Valley and parts of Glendale and Burbank, the dramatic nature of the debris flows and the disaster that followed captured the interest of the nation. This in turn focused attention on Southern California, a region that had been plagued by floods for decades because of poor leadership within the Los Angeles County Flood Control District. From its inception in 1914, flood control projects had been poorly planned and coordinated.

The appointment of E.C. Eaton as chief engineer in 1926 was a positive step for the Flood Control agency. Unfortunately, the chronic lack of funding hampered his ability to build vitally needed flood control projects. It was he who, after four years of toil, finally produced the first comprehensive plan for flood control involving the entire county from the mountains to the ocean. As fate would have it, it took the tragic New Year's Flood of 1934 to rally federal support for its implementation. Sadly, Eaton became the scapegoat for the '34 flood and resigned under fire.

In July of that year, President Roosevelt authorized the use of $13.9 million from the Works Progress Administration (WPA) to finance a number of high-priority projects in Eaton's comprehensive plan. (The WPA replaced the hastily conceived CWA and became the largest public works employer in the nation.) The County of Los Angeles provided $3.5 million for land purchases. The work was supervised by the U.S. Army Corps of Engineers using locals on the WPA relief rolls. Over sixteen thousand worked on deepening and widening the Los Angeles River. Hundreds toiled in the Crescenta Valley, building debris basins and cement-lined flood control channels that emptied into Verdugo Creek (twelve and a half miles of flood channels).

The Flood Control Act of 1936 expanded the power of the U.S. Army Corps of Engineers beyond most people's imagination. Henceforth, the corps would have sole authority in providing flood control on all of the nation's rivers and streams. It provided massive expenditures for fifty flood control projects throughout the nation. Last, but certainly not least, 25 percent of the money was allocated to Los Angeles County alone. For the next twenty years, most of the money expended for flood projects in Los Angeles would be funneled through the Corps of Engineers.

In general, engineers, civic leaders and private citizens applauded the Army Corps' efforts to make Eaton's comprehensive plan a reality. There was no malice at all aimed at the U.S. government. In fact, there were many in the engineering community who wished it had taken place decades earlier.

11

REFORESTATION V. DEBRIS BASINS

The Army Corps of Engineers Wins

The organization is strong in its conviction that the building of proper check dams, reforestation and other methods of flood control is the solution of the problem. Its officers claim the debris basin construction would prove a waste of the taxpayers' money, and would prove a menace to life and health.
—*from the* Crescenta Valley Ledger, *writing about the meeting of an anti-debris basin group*

During the height of the great flood of '34, one unintentional flood control project functioned surprisingly well. It was an empty sand and gravel pit at the foot of Haines Canyon. This canyon encompasses about one and a half square miles (about the size of Pickens Canyon) and drains into the Tujunga Wash. During the violent discharge of rocks and debris that night, it filled to the brim, trapping the debris and forcing the excess water to spill out and flow harmlessly downhill. In terms of shape and capacity, it provided the flood control engineers with a workable prototype. The consensus at the time was that it saved a good part of Tujunga from severe damage.

When County Flood Control and the U.S. Army Corps of Engineers made public its plans to build, from east to west, seven similar debris or catchment basins above the valley, a small opposition group spoke out. Barely two months after the flood, the *Ledger* wrote of "opposition voiced by owners of estates above Foothill Blvd." They believed that the debris basins "would be a menace to life and health." Their main fear was that the basins would "depreciate the value of their property." They, in turn, sided with conservationists who insisted on reforestation and the rebuilding of the failed check dams. They were correct on one issue. Debris basins did have to be "re-gouged," or emptied, of accumulated debris from time to time.

The Corps of Engineers, in particular, turned a deaf ear to their lament. They were acutely aware that burned-over slopes increased runoff, more than twenty or thirty fold. But they refused to rely on check dams and mustard seed again. They also knew that in the last flood, from Pomona to Topanga, canyons heavily forested produced significant debris flows as well. The Geologic Survey of 1937 states about the Flood of 1934, "The discharge of water into Glendale and Burbank from canyons draining southern and western slopes of the Verdugo Mountains and San Rafael Hills was torrential and heavily loaded with debris, although these slopes had normal forest cover." If this is the case, the San Gabriel chain must pose an even greater threat on its forested slopes. In short, fires are not always responsible for the intensity of the flow. Gigantic boulders were strewn all over this valley prior to the fire and flood of 1933 and 1934. We can assume that many of those boulders were washed down without fires preceding them.

The fairly gentle slopes of the Verdugo Mountains provide an interesting example of flooding on forested slopes during the New Year's deluge of 1934. An account of this event was shared, which focused on Brand Canyon, located in these mountains on the south slope in Glendale (near Burbank). This eyewitness account appeared in a letter written by a hydrology engineer (one who specializes in the movement of water in relation to land). According to him, this area had not been subjected to any fire since 1928. Meanwhile, a number of check dams had been constructed throughout the canyon. He gives a vivid description of the debris flow as it surged down the forested canyon a few minutes after midnight:

> Boulders weighing several tons were carried down a distance of over a mile from the mouth of the canyon. Autos parked on Western Ave. were rolled over and over until they were a mass of wreckage. At Kenneth Road and Western Avenue 2 autos were buried in mud until only 6 inches of the tops were visible. A 5-room frame house, a mile from the canyon, was washed 300 feet from its foundation. The street car tracks on Glenoaks Boulevard were buried from 2 to 3 feet for a distance of several thousand feet... Neighbors say it hit at midnight with a terrible roar.

On January 7, the engineer climbed up the ravaged canyon and discovered that seventeen out of the nineteen check dams were partially or completely destroyed. He also wrote, "I found a tree where the bark had been entirely removed at least 9 feet above the ground surface. The width of the stream channel at this point was approximately 40 feet." Is it any wonder that the Corps of Engineers and members of County Flood Control concluded that forested slopes were not impervious to mud slides and debris flows if it rained hard enough or long enough? The engineers also insisted that "check dams were and are an extravagance and a menace."

In spite of some contrarians soon after the flood, community leaders had embraced the concept of debris basins to capture the rocks, boulders and broken trees while allowing the de-silted water to flow freely down the flood channels. Loans from the Reconstruction Finance Corporation were needed to start construction. Unfortunately, it took some time for the County Flood Control District to resolve certain financial restrictions. Once this was accomplished, work was started at the base of Hall Beckley and Pickens Canyons. More federal funds were forthcoming when Congress passed legislation in 1935 and 1936.

On January 25, 1935, the *Ledger* featured a story on the "rally" held at the Hall Beckley Debris Basin site. A crowd of two hundred people journeyed up the hill to inspect a work in progress. Chief Engineer Fisher explained how the basin separated the debris and silt from the rushing waters before it was released to continue its course to the Verdugo Wash, "With the removal of the silt and debris, the water is robbed of a big percentage of its menace." The crowd was assured that it was not a dam and that "there was nothing to break." Whatever flows over the spillway "is debris free" and posed no hazard on its controlled descent.

Haakon Berg, the highly respected president of the Crescenta-Cañada National Bank in Montrose, who led the fight for a Reconstruction Finance Corporation loan, told the audience that the battle was "about won." He expected legislative action on the matter "any day now." His optimistic prediction was made on January 25. A large allocation of $750,000 arrived five months later. Major work on Hall Beckley and Pickens Canyons was scheduled to begin on July 19, 1935. The last obstacle had been removed.

Once started, the work moved rapidly ahead. The Army Corps of Engineers used manpower from the WPA relief rolls. On September 6, the *Ledger* announced with pictures that work was "ahead of schedule" on both channels and basins.

Finally, on November 22, 1935, preparations were being made at the Oakmont Country Club for a grand fiesta celebrating the near completion of the debris basins and flood channels beneath the two canyons that released the most violent discharges nine minutes after midnight on January 1, 1934.

The final touches on the cement-lined flood channels were completed on November 29. Hall Beckley and Pickens flood channels are twenty-four feet across and twelve feet deep, capable of carrying the flows of two small rivers if need be. The other flood channels are twelve feet wide and twelve feet deep.

The Army Corps of Engineers opened operations in Eagle, Goss and Shields Canyons on September 20, 1936, with a deadline for completion on November 1, 1936. When completed, all three converged at Eagle debris basin and shared a common flood channel to the Verdugo Creek drainage.

Occasionally, problems emerged during construction. At one juncture, the Army Corps had planned on stopping all work as the rainy season approached. The property owners wanted no part of the cautionary attitude of the corps. This proposed delay also rankled the wage-poor laborers who were already working a shortened week. Outside pressure eventually led to a reversal of the corps' plan. It was decided that "if it rains and washes us out, then that will be just too bad, we'll have to start all over again." Homeowners and workers breathed a sigh of relief.

Finally, in February 1938, at a cost of $7,916,000 the county and federal government finished erecting a system of debris basins and flood channels unparalleled in the United States. To quote the ever-present *Ledger*, "Across the floor of the valley corrugating the alluvial fan at regular intervals, are debris basins and flood control channels capable of holding and controlling the flow of large rivers."

The plan relied on by the Corps of Engineers and County Flood Control dismissed the emphasis on reforestation and check dams. The chaparral would grow back, and the check dams were worthless. The engineers concentrated on gigantic debris basins and "great flumes" to carry the maximum amount of water away.

The plan worked well, and surprisingly, the massive holes in the ground did not irreparably scar the landscape. In fact, very few of the homeowners to this day have ever seen a debris basin or noticed a flood channel cutting under a street or passing over the 210 Freeway in its concrete corset.

Luckily, the valley's flood control infrastructure was completed in February 1938, because a month later, Los Angeles County was assaulted by the most destructive storm of the twentieth century. Unfortunately, the Army Corps of Engineers had just begun working below the foothills. Although the

Immediately after the flood, construction on an ambitious flood control system was begun. Concrete channels were put in place, generally following the flow of the '34 flood as houses had already been naturally cleared from those paths. *Courtesy of Joe and Linda Rakasits.*

At the mouth of each canyon is a debris basin (sometimes two or three in a series) designed to catch the larger rocks before they enter the concrete channels below. This is the Dunsmuir Debris Basin, at the mouth of Dunsmore Canyon (note the spelling discrepancy), just to the east of Deukmejian Wilderness Park.

The function of the debris basin is ingenious. The dam stops the debris flow long enough for the rocks to separate from the water. The bowl in the center catches those larger rocks and sediment, while the clear water continues into the concrete channels via the overflow outlet in the dam and the vertical perforated riser in the bowl. These basins need to be cleaned out on a regular basis.

worst flooding was in the San Fernando Valley, areas throughout this county experienced heavy damage. The city of Los Angeles lost all communications and relied solely on the radio to communicate. Railroads, bridges and highways were inundated. Over eighty people were killed in the county, and the destruction surpassed $70 million. Meanwhile, mountain gauges in the San Gabriels were recording from ten to eighteen inches of rain in one storm. And how did the Crescenta Valley fare? With an over-confident tone, the *Ledger* rejoiced, "The heavy rains and cloudburst...while filling the steep streets, drained harmlessly into the 'Mississippi Rivers' of concrete and steel that man built to stay, possibly forever, the hand of disaster..."

Today, there are 120 of these stadium-size debris basins located at the mouths of canyons along the entire south face of the San Gabriel Range. Over the years, tall perforated concrete towers have been installed in the center of these basins to accelerate the removal of the silt-free water from the basins to the flood channels. Beyond a doubt, the costly debris basins and flood control channels have proven their worth. They may have been "built to stay," but I take exception to the boast "forever." In the long course of history, humankind has usually fallen short in its duels with Nature.

12

ARE WE REALLY SAFE?

"Who's afraid of the big, bad flood!"
Certainly not the eighteen new families who moved into the Crescenta valley
last week!
—Crescenta Valley Ledger, *just after the flood*

For over four decades after the completion of the flood control projects, the Crescenta Valley was spared from any severe flooding. Collective amnesia had once more set in. Most newcomers had never heard of the New Year's Flood of 1934. Markridge, an east–west road about one and a quarter miles above Foothill Boulevard, was beginning to attract new homebuyers. In the late '50s, Bob and Jackie Genofile had built a beautiful home at the east end of Markridge, an acre of land that commanded a priceless view over the Verdugo Mountains to the Pacific Ocean. The pool was perfect for their children, Kimberlee and Scott. Above the house, a pristine wilderness of pine trees and mountain shrubbery greeted the eye. This vegetation carpeted a very steep slope along the mountain front. Surely, no one would attempt to build on that incline. Their idyllic existence was secure.

However, confidence and serenity were shattered in the mid-'60s when an ambitious developer purchased the steepened terrain and prepared to cover the wilderness area with stucco houses and concrete driveways. The contractor had no qualms about locating these new dwellings as close as possible to the mountainsides. Every potential site was leveled and built on.

One half mile up the slope from the Genofile home, a small dam and debris basin was constructed to capture the debris flows from the steep-walled Shields Canyon. The dam was too small and the debris basin was designed to hold a mere six thousand square yards of sediment. By contrast, the lower Shields debris basin beneath the Genofile home had a capacity of thirty-six thousand square yards. Prior to the housing boom, the canyon emptied itself onto an age-old alluvial fan, where it spread out in a natural progression at Nature's command. Pine Cone Road starts at a cul-de-sac below the dam and winds its way down the 41 percent grade, stopping abruptly on Markridge Road directly in front of the Genofile dream home.

This dream house was planned and built in 1958 by Bob Genofile, a general contractor who made his livelihood constructing school buildings, libraries and other public facilities. He personally supervised the work, making certain that the cinderblocks were properly connected with heavy steel rebar. Every hole was grouted with a proper mixture of cement and gravel. He wasn't anticipating a major mountain flood. It was just the way he constructed things.

In November 1975, a massive fire swept down on Sunland, Tujunga, La Crescenta and La Cañada. It was also a repeat of the Pickens Fire of November 1933 in that it burned off the southern face of the San Gabriel Mountains from Tujunga to La Cañada. However, this blaze destroyed 65,000 acres compared to the 1933 conflagration, which totaled 4,800 acres.

Three years later, after several wet winter months, a genuine "gully-washer" hit Los Angeles County on the night of February 9 and 10, 1978, when almost twelve inches of rain fell in twenty-four hours.

We live a quarter of a mile below the Genofiles on Harmony Place and will remember forever that torrential night. The sound of pelting rain kept us awake, and so we chose to watch it through the sliding glass doors in the den as it poured from our upper deck. Suddenly, at about 1:30 a.m., it turned into a solid sheet of water, not unlike a waterfall, lasting for at least twenty minutes. It was awesome to behold. We learned later that this intense downfall had triggered the devastating debris flow that had plunged down Pine Cone Road directly into the Genofile home. For the next three hours or more, the family of four would struggle to survive against a sodden invasion of black mud, rocks and boulders.

Preceding this rumbling mass down Pine Cone Road was a six-ton flood control truck with two men, racing to outrun the "black mass" at their rear bumper. They had arrived at the cul-de-sac just as the debris flow breached the small dam and quickly accelerated down the hill. By the narrowest of margins, they escaped the mountain's wrath.

On several occasions, Jackie Genofile, now a widow, and her son Scott have shared their memories of that fateful night with our local historical group. To this day, she has preserved her effervescent spirit in spite of the family's narrow brush with death. I know of no other family that experienced the frontal assault of a major debris flow and lived to tell about it. In spite of their material loss, God was on their side.

Jackie and daughter Kim were in Scott's room in front of the house looking up Pine Cone Road when they spotted what she called the "big black thing" coming down the hill. The "big black thing" was a massive debris flow filled with broken trees, boulders, mud and at least twelve automobiles when it crashed into their house. They all ran down the hall to the master bedroom, chased by a surging river of mud, rocks and trash. The parents climbed on the mattress, and they were gradually lifted to within a few feet of the ceiling. Prior to this, Bob had the good sense to kick out a glass door, which prevented the room from filling completely. Poor Scott and Kim were wedged between the railing of the bed and the wall with mud up to their chins. This all occurred within the first ten minutes. Once it stopped, they anticipated a timely rescue but were sorely disappointed. Rescue vehicles passed by but surmised that no one could have survived in the Genofile home. Hours later, Scott's persistent whistle finally alerted neighbors to their plight. Even then, it took some time to unearth the children. As it turned out, the Genofile family survived their ordeal with flying colors. With the exception of torn clothing and numerous debris-induced bruises, they were ready to face a new day. Jackie recalled, "We may have been cold and sore, but we sure didn't notice it."

With the light of day, they were able to see what the storm had wrought. The property resembled an auto-wrecking yard except that most of the vehicles were embedded in the mud, wrapped around trees or resting in the swimming pool. Daughter Kim's Camero was among the casualties. In the front of the house, mud and debris were twelve feet high, allowing walking access to the roof. The stench of wet earth was everywhere. The interior of the home was filled to the brim with hardening mud. But thanks to the building expertise of Mr. Robert Genofile, the structural integrity of his "fortress" was sound. Had the Genofile home been of the wood frame and stucco vintage, it would have been swept into the debris basin one hundred feet below.

There were other homes above the Genofiles' that sustained structural damage. Electrical, water and gas services were also disrupted. Last but not

The debris basins don't always work perfectly. In 1978, the Shields Canyon Debris Basin overflowed, sending tons of rocks and mud roaring down Pine Cone Road in the Pinecrest development. This is the Genofile house at Pine Cone and Markridge, buried up to the eaves in mud, rocks and wrecked cars.

least, a German shepherd that was washed away returned to its distraught owner, panting for affection.

A number of neighbors decided to relocate. They were in the minority. Most reckoned that the whole thing was an aberration.

The Genofiles opted for a lawsuit against the county. Enough evidence surfaced to convince the county that a $337,000 settlement was appropriate. The county also enlarged the dam and debris basin above the cul-de-sac on Pine Cone Road. The debris basin was increased from 6,000 to 40,200 cubic yards. Had this been done in the first place, the Genofile family would not be included among the luckiest of debris-flow survivors.

Soon after the flood, a neighbor commented on this remarkable family: "They are courageous people. One day they had it all, and the next day it was ripped away from them." Perhaps the neighbor thought that they were ready to abandon their dream house. Not a chance! Once they were assured that Bob's "fortress" had passed the ultimate structural test, they decided to rebuild with a passion. Not wishing to tempt fate, the wise father and husband added a second story and moved all of the bedrooms to that level. They were back in the remodeled abode within seven months while the finishing touches were being added. From time to time, they would make some pleasant discoveries. While playing in the lower Shields debris basin, Scott spotted a glint of something in a clear pool of water. It proved to be his mother's diamond ring! And fifteen years later, Jackie's trustworthy gardener found her old purse partially buried in the rose garden with her money still intact. These were small things but helped a little with the healing. Sadly, Kim never found even one of her Barbie doll collection, nor did Scott unearth a single Hot Wheels car.

I called Jackie Genofile in late July 2012 at the "house that Bob built" and was pleased to hear her delightful voice again. It still matches her effervescent personality. She leads a full life and enjoys her balcony in the sky. Two K-rails (set in place to divert debris and floodwater) remain in front of her home as a special precaution since the Station Fire of 2009. For thirty-four years, the regouged upper Shields debris basin has served the community well.

And so, the question still remains: "Are we really safe?" I believe that we, in the Crescenta Valley, are reasonably safe, thanks to the Army Corps of Engineers and the Los Angeles County Flood Control.

It is obvious to us now that the upper Shields debris basin was far too shallow to trap even moderate debris flows. Someone clearly miscalculated. Since then, County Flood Control has completely rebuilt the debris basin. For three and a half decades, there have been no debris basin failures.

We must also remember that we chose to live in a flood-prone area. An engineer for the Army Corps' Southern California office said in 2003, "These basins are built to withstand the largest flows that the corps expects... They are built to reasonably minimize the risk of damage within economic constraints." Lest we forget, debris basins have been known to fail. "It can happen and it has happened...but the degree of damage has been within acceptable tolerance." (Unless it is your house!)

In February 1978, a week after the Shields Canyon debacle, I took a picture of the Eagle Canyon debris basin just below the Pinecrest community (capacity: 63,100 cubic yards). Shields and Goss Canyons also empty into this massive bowl. To casual observers, the basin appeared to have reached close to its maximum capacity. Another storm or succession of storms could have caused an overflow, endangering homes on the west side of Two Strike Park and below. Fortunately, there was a respite between storms, allowing Flood Control personnel to truck most of the debris to sediment placement sites.

The very expression "sediment placement site" arouses vehement criticism among some valley homeowners, especially those living beneath these ever-growing mounds of ashen earth. They are also irritated by the noisy dump-trucks transporting this material to designated sites. At least, the truck drivers are content with lucrative seasonal business.

At 11:00 a.m. on February 10, 1978, while the Genofile family was still recuperating from their ordeal, a saturated section from a large sediment placement site below Dunsmore Canyon slid down and into the homes on Markridge Road. Over three hundred volunteers helped the Flood Control workers respond to the distress call.

In fairness to the engineers, where pray should they have transported the waste excavated from the debris basins? Frankly, no one knows where to put it. No feasible solution has yet been discovered. And as our quest goes on, so too does our frustration.

The county has done its best to resolve these problems with the tools at its disposal. It contends with a great deal of undeserved public criticism. At present, the engineers are developing a novel method to secure the sediment sites. As one drives up to the top of Dunsmore Avenue, a formidable dome of compacted debris comes into view. It was trucked in from foothill debris basins that filled up in the flooding that followed the Station Fire in August 2009. The story of this innovation appeared in the *Glendale News Press* in September 2011 as the project was getting underway. The subtitle read, "Sediment Placement Area Will Be Adorned with Vegetation to Avoid Runoff." It was designed "to better anchor" the controversial Dunsmore sediment placement site. The amount to be anchored comes to about 500,000 cubic yards. Geotechnical experts believe that the new landscaping plan "will bring the most stability to the sediment dome." One critic commented, "I would like to see the whole thing trucked out!" And I say, "Show me the money!" It will already cost the county $500,000 by the time landscaping is finished in 2013. Experts estimate that it will take fifteen years for the monkey flower, sagebrush and deer weed to fully mature. I, for one, salute their efforts and pray for success.

EPILOGUE

And over all the California sunshine is giving a note of cheerfulness and lending encouragement to the flood sufferers who are carrying on.
—Crescenta Valley Ledger, *just after the flood*

Let's remember, it was optimism and true grit that made this valley an ideal place to live and raise our families. Every environment offers its share of challenges and disappointments. We will always have to cope with the vagaries of Mother Nature.

The Crescenta Valley certainly had its share of plucky realtors. Four days after the New Year's flood, a gardener/ realtor, W.P. Davis, was touting the advantages of flood silt. He wrote in a local paper that it contained rock phosphate for fruit blossoms and nitrogen for lawn growth, "just spade it into the garden and around the shrubbery."

Frank and Lillian Green opened their new real estate office a few months into 1934. They were undaunted even though the Hall Beckley debris flow had destroyed their home and previous office. Her real estate listings were washed away. Their ad read, "We thank the public for past patronage and hope...to be doing a larger business in the future." Her green office was still standing on the southwest corner of Ocean View and Glenada Avenues when I was a teenager in the 1940s.

Mark Collins predicted a big housing boom in 1935, second only to that of the 1920s. All of his rentals were taken.

One writer (name unknown) started his pitch with: "Who's afraid of the big, bad flood?" He admitted that there were "quite a number" of

The legacy these natural floods have left the Crescenta Valley are the tons of natural building material available below our feet. Stone construction is the native architectural style locally, and the best example is St. Luke's Church at Rosemont and Foothill Boulevard. The valley is often called "Rock Crescenta" by those forced to do any digging in our rocky soil.

families who "left these parts" immediately after the flood, but "they too are beginning to return." He concluded, "Once we get a taste of the valley, we just can't leave it for long. The writer knows. He tried it!"

This does not mean that potential homebuyers lost all caution at purchase time. Most sought locations that were safe from future floods. "Flood Proof Lots" were high on their list. Rental ads stressed "Out of Flood Zone." This, of course, was prior to the completion of the debris basins and flood channels in 1938.

There are those who, once they settled in our valley, never had an inclination to leave. Then there were those who came here on extended visits, longed to return and did so.

One of those who satisfied his longing to return to this area was Nick Virgallito, who first visited here in 1933 as a teenager with his Civilian Conservation Corps company. They were stationed in Earl Canyon at the top of Palm Drive in La Cañada. While there, he fought the great Pickens Fire of November 1933, built check dams in the canyons and assisted in body recovery after the New Year's Flood of 1934. Several months later, his CCC company was overjoyed to return to the green hills of Ohio. But Nick always had a special place in his heart for our valley. In 1938, he left Ohio with his bride and eventually raised a family of four in California. Nick is now in his nineties but looks a handsome sixty and lives in La Crescenta on Rockdale Avenue.

In 1915, we were privileged to have an internationally renowned artist settle in our midst. His name was Seymour Thomas. He married the lovely Helen Haskell, who had once been the valley's first schoolteacher in 1887. Thomas was known as a painter of presidents, statesmen and scientists. His portrait of Woodrow Wilson presently hangs in the East Wing of the White House. Although always in demand for his painting skills, he found time to play an active role in the community and personally designed St. Luke's of the Mountains Episcopal Church. Legend has it that he marked many special stones in the area that were used in its construction. His painting of the proposed sanctuary may be seen in the church office. When asked why he still lived here, Thomas wrote, "I spent years traveling around the world searching for the best place to live. I looked for a climate advantage in every country on the globe, and when I returned, I found it right here where I had started from—in the Crescenta Valley."

CLOSURE

It's just as vivid today whenever it starts raining.
—Marcie Warfield Flannery

Prior to World War II, the locals still shared memories of the '34 flood. The names of those who perished, old and young alike, often came up in casual conversations. There was talk for a while of building a permanent memorial to honor the victims. For some reason, it never came to fruition, even though it might have provided closure for some. After 1945, a new world emerged, and January 1, 1934, became lost in the current of time.

Shortly after the Historical Society of the Crescenta Valley was founded in June 2002, a number of active members began resurrecting the valley's past. The forgotten story of the 1934 flood caught our attention. Several of us proposed mounting a bronze memorial plaque on a cairn constructed with local rocks, honoring those who lost their lives just minutes after midnight on January 1, 1934.

The county granted a permit to build on the northeast corner of Rosemont and Fairway Avenues, just below the original site of the American Legion Hall. Look for the sycamore tree that Tob Lamar leaped into when the debris flow smashed through the Legion post. It still stands, tall and proud.

Stuart Byles designed and supervised the construction of the cairn. Mike Lawler and Art Cobery dug the hole, groomed the soil and fetched the rocks.

On January 1, 2004, the morning brought forth blue skies and bright sunlight. The flag was displayed, and a beautiful array of flowers surrounded the rock cairn. A single long-stemmed red rose rested on the bronze plaque.

On New Years Day 2004, the seventieth anniversary of the flood, a monument was dedicated at the intersection of Fairway and Rosemont, just yards from the former site of the American Legion Hall. Flood survivors attended and shared memories. *Left to right*: Bob Lorenz, Jane Mosher-Usher, Mark Higley (son of Lee Higley), Amy Kelly, Eloise Benson Nicholl (standing), Malcolm Benson (hidden), Charles Bausback and Maureen Perry. *Photo by Art Cobery.*

We were pleasantly surprised to see 130 people gathered for the dedication. Several members of the historical society briefed the onlookers on the significance of the tragic New Year's Flood of 1934.

Seven venerable flood survivors were comfortably seated on the right side of the cairn and plaque. They came to share their poignant stories with friends and neighbors alike concerning an event that forever changed their lives. As each spoke, the audience listened with rapt attention. Four members of this select group of survivors are included within the pages of this book: Malcolm Benson, Eloise Benson Nicholl, the late Chuck Bausback and Bob Lorenz.

A younger man sitting with the survivors that morning was Mark Higley, who came to speak on behalf of his father, Lee Higley, who could not bear to speak of that sad night. Lee and his sister, Barbara, ages eight and six, respectively, lost their mother and father in a matter of seconds when the Pickens Canyon debris flow destroyed their home on Encinal Avenue. Lee Higley, a man in his eighties, carries that heavy loss to this very day. With that said, he deeply appreciates that the community honors the memory of those who perished on that black New Year's morning.

Hopefully, the small monument on Rosemont and Fairway Avenues affords some sense of closure for those who still remember.

FLOOD STORIES AND EYEWITNESS ACCOUNTS

The Ananda Ashrama was a religious retreat located at the top of Pennsylvania Avenue. The residents of the Ashrama sent letters about the flood to their sister center in Massachusetts. This is an excerpt from Swami Paramananda's letter to Boston from La Crescenta a couple days after the event:

A flood was anticipated because of the recent terrible fire which burned to the ground all the growth over 6,000 acres of mountain area. The destruction of natural watershed was regarded as a great menace to the safety of the people in the valley in case of heavy rainfall, but one, even with the most far-reaching eye, could not have foreseen what actually took place on New Year's Eve on 1933–1934. A gentle rain started two days prior to this and by Sunday, December 31st, great streams of water rushed down from the mountain canyons.

Not until the bells announced the New Year at midnight did the great crisis come. Great rocks and boulders weighing between 500–100,000 pounds rolled down with unimagined speed, carrying with them giant oak trees, brush and debris on a high tide of water. People were reveling in New Year's festivities...homes, cars on the roads...all unaware of the danger. Roads once smooth, paved highways no longer existed, walking was impossible. For the first few days, one couldn't walk even a few steps without sinking into mud.

Heroic men and women of the Red Cross and Welfare Societies of cities and counties labored day and night to alleviate the suffering. Mules carried water buckets from house to house.

From a recent interview with flood survivor Marcie Warfield Flannery:

It's just as vivid today whenever it starts raining.

We'd had a pretty good Christmas that year. It was '33, and we were still in somewhat of a depression. My dad had finally had a pretty good paycheck, and we had a Christmas tree. I was eleven; I had a younger brother, Buddy, six years old, and I had my older brother, Charles, probably thirteen. We'd lost my mom a year or so before, and we had a housekeeper, Genevieve Wood, and her daughter, Edith, maybe four.

One of the things we didn't get to do—Dad had promised us—if the rain stopped and it was a good day, he was going to take us down to see the Rose Parade. We'd never seen it. We got to stay up late; we didn't have TV and a lot of things, but we were excited that we got to stay up.

It had been raining for a week, and for three days we had heard rocks rolling down Rosemont. The newspaper said that in twenty-four hours we had had thirteen inches of rain, and we could hear the boulders and whatever other debris going down the boulevard like marbles. In the late afternoon of the thirty-first, I think my dad began to really get concerned. He'd been watching it for three days. He must have walked down to Rosemont because when he came back he said, "We can't get out. I can't get the car out. We'd never make it." So we just stayed there in the front room. I remember closer to midnight the housekeeper saying, "Let's pray," and we started saying the Lord's Prayer.

Then the house started really shaking. Now, the house we lived in—I'm sure we didn't own it, we were probably renting—was just a little wood frame, probably two or three bedrooms, just a little bungalow. We could hear things hit the house. Sandbags or anything else would not have helped us. I was standing next to Genevieve in our little hallway, and I turned to look at my little bedroom clear at the back of the house. I was going to run back and get a doll, or my little treasure box. I had this little treasure box that had one ear ring from my great-grandmother and my mother's cameo. My mother died when I was nine, so this was all I had. I was going to run back and get these because I didn't know what was going to happen. I turned and took maybe one step, and the wall—it's hard to explain, it's like an avalanche as high as the house. It came over us and swept us all in. The house was smashed like kindling wood, and we went down with it.

I went down fighting as anyone would, struggling to stay alive. You weren't fighting water, you were fighting boulders and automobiles. I was conscious the whole time. I remember trying to get out and trying to breathe. It was rocks and mud, and I was trying to grab anything, and things were moving at a pretty fast rate. I grabbed onto the tail of a big animal. I don't remember anyone having cows, but I do remember horses. The tail was too long and too big for a dog, so it had to be a horse. I grabbed onto this tail, and it saved my life. Maybe that horse was struggling to stay alive as well, maybe it was dead, but I was holding on to its tail. It got me over to the side of the flood.

Somebody knew how bad the situation was up there, and they had sent some CCC boys up in the area. Miraculously, there were two or three young men by the side, and they grabbed me and pulled me out of the mire. They carried me to the American Legion Hall and up the steps past the railing. We got inside the hall, and it seemed like everyone was naked! Your clothes were ripped off by the flood—everything was ripped off. They had used anything they had to cover the people—paper bags and newspapers. I was eleven years old, and I was a very shy little girl, and I was cold and full of mud.

When they took me into the Legion Hall, there was an upright piano. I saw my dad. He was across from me—they had just brought me in. I saw him, and he had Edith in one arm and my little brother in the other arm, and I

The interior of the American Legion Hall the next day shows that the flood had swept the inside clear of furniture and people. Despite the violence of the maelstrom, the drapes, wall hangings and light fixtures are eerily undisturbed.

remember an upright piano toward the back wall. I remember hearing—it had to be a Red Cross worker—I don't know if they had a switchboard or just a phone—I remember a lady saying, "Mayday! Mayday! Mayday! Do you hear me? Mayday!" And about that time, the building started shaking. I was just about to walk over to my dad when I looked up, and this wall of mud was coming. It came through the back wall—I'm estimating fifteen feet of mud broke down that wall. I remember that mud coming. It wasn't like clear water, like Niagara Falls. I'm talking automobiles and houses that had become kindling. I remember my dad yelling something to me like, "Run, Marcie!" I saw the piano get pushed across the floor, and it crushed my dad, and he went out with the piano and the wall behind him. I remember grabbing for a rail—you were grabbing anything to survive. Either I was torn off the rail or I went down with the rail. I must have lost consciousness because I do not remember anything—struggling to stay alive, fighting anybody, grabbing anything. I don't know how long I was unconscious. I have no idea what time it was, but when I came to it was totally dark. I was in—I've since called it a cocoon—I wasn't buried. I crawled out from under a huge rock or something. I got myself standing. I was knee deep in mud. As I looked around, it was like what I later saw in video broadcasts from the moon landings. It was like a flat colorless moonscape, nothingness—I didn't recognize anything.

I was wet, naked, cold, full of mud. I didn't know how badly I was injured. I don't remember feeling pain. I heard crying. I could hear moaning and crying way in the distance. I remember I heard this particular moan and then a cry, and I said, "Buddy, Buddy, is that you Buddy?" and he started crying. Then I heard my dad saying, "Marcie, is that you? Where are you?" I said, "Daddy, keep talking! I can't see you! Where are you? Keep talking so I can find you." I finally spotted him. I don't know how far away he was, but he was moaning, and I could tell he finally passed out. Meanwhile, my little brother was still crying. The miraculous thing is how we three were in a radius, maybe the size of a house. I was looking around thinking, "What do I do?" when I spotted a little two-door coupe, and I thought maybe I can get in there. I made my way over there and saw that it was buried halfway, so I dug the mud away from both doors. I then went and got my dad into the car. I'm not sure how I did it as he was six feet tall, 185 pounds and his hip was shattered. He couldn't have walked. I don't know if I carried him or if he crawled and I helped him—I just don't remember.

Then I said, "Buddy, where are you, honey?" I located him, and he was buried up to his neck. I thought his head was just another rock. I dug him out and got him in the car. I got in with them and tried to figure out what to do. I

When the sun rose the next morning in a beautiful cloudless sky, what had been neighborhoods was now a moonscape. The view is looking down the Pickens Canyon channel toward Rosemont and Montrose Avenues.

got out of the car again and dug the mud away from the headlights. I got in and honked the car's horn and flashed the headlights until the battery went dead. By that time, it was breaking dawn, and I remember saying something to my dad like: "Daddy, we made it" or "Daddy, we're alive." He was just out—he was in bad shape.

I looked out through the windshield and saw three men coming toward us, and they said that they had seen the lights flashing. Two of the men carried my dad, and one carried my little brother, but there wasn't anyone to carry me, so I walked with them. We were walking in two feet of mud. It wasn't a nice flat surface, and you sunk in with every step. I don't know how far we went, but we had to get to where the ambulances could get us. I felt no pain—I didn't know that I was injured. I had mud in my mouth, my ears, my eyes, my entire body. I learned later when I was at the hospital that I had been packed with mud, that the force of the water had literally impacted me with mud. I had a broken ankle on my left leg and a puncture wound almost all the way through my right knee. My right foot was almost totally crushed. The mud was a good thing in a way. It acted as a packing, like in that hole

125

It could have been this car that the Warfield family sheltered in. Hundreds of cars like this were mired in the mud. Some people were trapped in them, and others took refuge in them.

that was almost clear through my knee. It kept it from bleeding. And my foot that was totally smashed—probably if it had not been caked in mud, I would have lost a lot more blood.

My older brother was found later, but he didn't have severe damage. He didn't go down twice, he only went down the once from the house. We didn't know if he was dead or alive for three weeks. You see, we were all taken to different hospitals. They had ambulances waiting in a certain area, and people were out trying to rescue people. My brother ended up in Glendale. My dad and younger brother, even though we were all three together, ended up at Good Samaritan, and I was sent to the County Hospital in Los Angeles.

My father was left with one leg shorter than the other and always had a pretty severe limp after that. He was always in pain. He was killed in an automobile accident in 1938. I don't know who told me this or if it was in the paper, but Genevieve, the housekeeper, her body was found wrapped around a telephone pole. And her daughter, Edith—they only found half her body. My older brother was washed down farther—I don't know how far—and someone took him to the Glendale hospital. He didn't really talk about it that much, and my dad didn't talk about it much. And I didn't either until I was in my eighties.

CHILD HEROINE OF MONTROSE RECOVERING
Eleven-Year-Old Girl Saves Unconscious Father and Brother

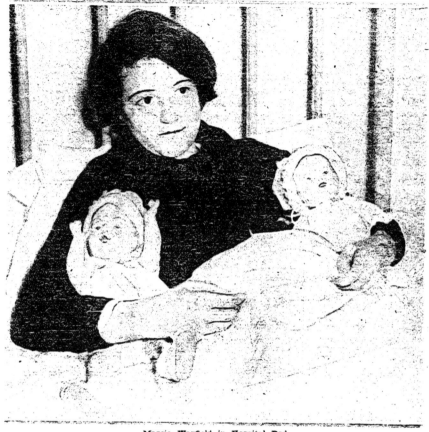

Marcia Warfield in Hospital Bed

Eleven-year-old Marcia Warfield was a national hero after the disaster. This photo is from the front page of the *Los Angeles Times* a few days after the flood. The dolls were given to her by nurses at the hospital, as little Marcie had lost everything. She repressed most of her memories of the tragedy soon after this.

It just amazes me all the time that an eleven-year-old girl could do what I had done. It feels like I'm telling the story of some other little girl. Every time I read about it or talk about it, I think, "How did I do it?"

AUTHOR'S NOTE: Marcie was released from the hospital in 1934. The Red Cross set her and her family up in an apartment in Los Angeles. They never

Eighty-eight-year-old Marcie Warfield Flannery sits at her dining room table in 2010 looking at newspaper clippings and letters from that long-buried portion of her life. Despite the time lapse, her memories are disturbingly vivid. Seventy-five years after the flood, she still gets nervous every time it rains. *Photo by Art Cobery.*

came back to the Crescenta Valley, as there was nothing to come back for. Their house and their belongings had been totally destroyed. Marcie said in her recollection that she and her father and brothers never talked much about the incident. When her father died in 1938, the family, and the collective memory of their experiences, was further fragmented. Marcie found it easier to put the whole experience behind her, so she never mentioned it again to her husband or her daughter.

A few years ago, she was reminded of the incident as anniversaries of the disaster made the news media. She finally told the story to a friend, who in turn encouraged her to tell her story to others. Just last year, she reached out to the Historical Society of the Crescenta Valley. We recorded the interview you read above. She related that she had not been back to the Crescenta Valley since that night, and she expressed a desire to return before she dies.

We were able to give her a tour of the sites of that horrible tragedy. We took her to the flood control channel on Mayfield that had been the site of her house in 1933 and to the American Legion Hall. Much of the time she was speechless, and her eyes were filled with tears. In the Legion Hall, she was able to stand right where her dad had been when she saw him crushed by the piano, and she grabbed on to and straddled the railing that she had clutched as she was swept out the front of the hall. Later that day, we united her with other living survivors of that night who had all been children like her. She was able to hold their hands and reconnect with a part of her life that had been buried for seventy-five years.

The author of this letter was previously unknown, but it was recently discovered to have been written by Helen Casey. The letter contains many wild exaggerations that were commonly reported at the time:

As it approached midnight I made a pot of coffee and some sandwiches and poured some Kimmel to toast the New Year. We finished our snack and stood to toast the New Year at the stroke of midnight, then started to dance together to the music of the radio.

Suddenly, at 12:02 a.m., there was a roaring rush of water, such as I never heard this side of Niagara. Billy dropped me and jumped to the window exclaiming, "I don't like the sound of that." As he spoke, all the lights went out and of course the radio went dead.

He ran past me into the bedroom throwing off his dressing gown and I ran into the kitchen to get some candles. Just then the phone rang.

"This flood is getting dreadful, there's four feet of water rushing past our gate—I'm getting frightened," my friend Helen Walker said.

I said, "It isn't that bad here yet, come on over," and she said, "Frank has gone out to see how things look—I'll wait for him," and hung up.

I lit candles and carried them into the front room. Bill was getting into his storm clothes. The phone rang again and again it was Helen, crying bitterly. She said, "I can't find Frank, he's been washed away, there's nothing but rushing water—Frank's gone!"

I said that Billy would be right over and hung up. I turned to Bill. "Go over and get Helen but come right back. There's nothing you can do. Please come right back."

He grabbed a flashlight, said, "Don't worry, Babe," and ran out. I dashed back to the phone to tell Helen he was on his way, but, between then and the time she had phoned me, the phone had gone dead. I ran out on the porch to see if I could see his flashlight but there was nothing but pitch blackness and the roar of the water.

I came back in the house and wandered around from room to room. My pet, Scoots, was under the kitchen table, whimpering softly.

It was almost a half hour later before I heard Billy call me. For a moment I was too weak to move, then I jumped up and ran out on the porch in time to see him and Walker struggling up the path with a limp figure between them. I thought it was Helen but it proved to be Mrs. Anderson, who had taken over Fisher's Grove a few months before. A five-foot wall of water had come right through one wall and out the other, carrying her—and all the furniture—with it. She had landed in a clump of oaks and managed to cling there and finally to climb one of the trees—she is in her 50s and stout.

In the meantime, Billy was wandering around hunting for Walker when he heard her faint call for help. Frederick Street was a raging torrent and there was nothing for him to do but leap across it in order to reach her. He did so and of course the bank of the far side caved in under him. As he went down a boulder or timber struck him on the knee, throwing him off balance and he went under, being swept down about a hundred feet before he managed to catch hold of some roots of a fir tree and drag himself out. By the time he reached her she had slipped out of the tree and was lying in the water under it, nearer dead than alive.

In the meantime Walker had been up on Mayfield seeing if anyone needed help. He saw Bill's flashlight and came down to see who it was and between them they managed to get her back across Frederick and up to the house—although all three were almost swept away in the effort.

The poor soul had on a corselet and parts of her dress; everything else had been torn off, shoes, stockings—even her false teeth were washed away. She was badly scratched and bruised but not seriously injured. I dried her off as well as I could and wrapped her in blankets and gave her a good stiff drink, then made a big pot of coffee.

In the meantime, Billy and Walker had gone over to get poor Helen at last—alone in her house all this time. When the three of them came back we all drank coffee royales and smoked cigarettes until the air was blue and tried to cheer each other up with "I think it's let up a little," "It doesn't seem as bad as it was," "I guess the worst is over," etc. We said this at the top of our lungs to be heard over the roar of the storm and none of us in the least sure we were right. I noticed Bill was limping a little and taxed him with it, which was when he admitted a rock had hit him, but it was "nothing."

We didn't get much sleep that night for we were all strung up from the flood. When I came to start the coffee I found there was no water—the pipes had burst. I put pans out and easily caught enough rain water to do for a sketchy wash. I cleaned up a bit, everything was covered with mud and candle grease.

About 3 p.m. the lights and radio came on, and we learned our first details of what had happened and how lucky we had really been. The first reports we heard said there were 17 dead and several missing as well as considerable property damage. (Neither they nor we yet dreamed that there were almost 300 dead and literally scores of homes washed away.)

In the afternoon I walked down to Pennsylvania Avenue to see how things looked from there. When I reached Pennsylvania Avenue I could scarcely believe my eyes. My astonishment started at New York Avenue which, from the south side of Montrose Avenue on down to the wash, was literally gone. It was just a gaping hole anywhere from 5 to 10 feet deep with twisted bits of water and gas pipes sticking up here and there.

Montrose Avenue was covered with mud and debris to a depth of at least six feet above the normal street level. The Trading Post was completely washed away. The whole front of Mac's Garage was caved in and the whole building in a state of collapse. Watley's Service Station at Pennsylvania and Honolulu was gone too. Jennings house was still standing, although the water had swept through it. The house next to it was gone entirely—three died there. Everybody was just standing around looking dazed. We couldn't think of what to do.

I had seen enough for one dose and didn't go any further. Besides, it was starting to rain again. That evening the radio had the death list up to 40.

Wrecked cars were prolific after the flood. This car was wrapped around a telephone pole on Montrose Avenue. *Courtesy of Joe and Linda Rakasits.*

Billy was very quiet but insisted he was all right. Fortunately I had enough canned goods in the house to feed us. We were running very shy of drinking water so we didn't drink much. The next morning, a Red Cross tank truck came through the street with water and I got a five-gallon jar filled. They came through every day after that.

Billy later wanted to take a walk and look things over for himself. We walked down as far as Rosemont and the things we saw were ghastly. On Montrose, they were digging a car out of the middle of the street, its roof at least a foot under the street level of mud and debris. There were five bodies in it.

They were shoveling mud out of the second story windows of Rockhaven Sanatorium; there were nine patients and two nurses lost there. A large white angora goat was lying by the gate, drowned, washed from heaven knows where. Pleasant Way was gone—some time later they sent surveyors up with a plat map to try and discover where the five houses on that one block had stood. There weren't even foundations left.

Some of our friends and a great many of our acquaintances were killed; Mrs. Kahn and Mrs. Myrtle Adams, the Wilson family except the 8-year-old boy—the mother and small baby were never even found. Mrs. Correa's boy, Higbee, was found weeks later floating in San Pedro Harbor. He had been washed away from Rosemont and Altura. Many were listed as missing who were never found; their bones will probably be dug up years from now or else they were washed clear out to sea. All but one wall of the American Legion Hall was swept away and 35 bodies were lost there, refugees who had been brought up from lower ground earlier in the evening. The whole thing was absolutely ghastly and almost impossible to believe.

It was five days before they had a road open to Glendale and then only with a resident's permit. The American Legion patrolled the roads day and night to prevent possible looting, although there wasn't much one could loot; everything had been washed away. The newspapers got the death list up to 47 and called it quits—in reality there were 284 death certificates signed in Montrose alone. All the reporters admitted privately that the situation was a great deal worse than the Long Beach earthquake—more deaths, more injured and more property damage.

Sparr Heights Hall was turned into Red Cross Headquarters and they took instant and complete charge and as usual did wonderful work. On account of Billy being hurt I couldn't very well leave the house much for the first four days, but as soon as I could I offered my services.

Glendale had a heavy toll too. All the bridges were washed away as far south as Brand, those across the wash, and at Central and Pacific. There were a number killed in that section, also down around Glenoaks Boulevard in the northwest part of town.

This is a picture of true desperation. This home near Verdugo Road and Opechee Way is barely being held up from sliding into the Verdugo Creek bed.

A letter from Charles Crowe, 3023 Prospect Avenue, to his mother and sister in Iowa:

Dear Mother, Frances & All:

It was just a week ago that a six foot wall of water hit our home and here we are alive and able to recount our terrible experience. It started raining Sat. noon and came down continuously until Monday noon. Sunday evening Mr. and Mrs. Harbin and Mrs. Fisher, a lady about 80 years old, felt uneasy in their home and came over to our place to spend the night which was New Year's Eve. The young couple next door came over also and we played games till 10 o'clock. Kirk and Victor went over with the young couple and prepared to stay with them over night to make room for the 3 other people. They thought it quite a lark. We retired, Bobby with Hazel and I; and Mrs. Harbin who is helpless from the hips down and her husband retired to the rear bedroom. Grandma Fisher slept on the davenport.

It was just 12 midnight, New Year's Eve when Hazel and I bounced out of bed when we were awakened by a terrific roaring like continuous thunder. As I hit the floor my feet struck ice cold water and mud. I looked in towards the front room when a great wall of water, boulders, rock and sand struck the front of the house tearing the front door off with the casing and in just a second we were above our knees in water and sand. We could hardly hear each other as Hazel tried to make for the door and I called her back. I was terrified but tried to keep my head. The first thing that I thought of was to let the torrent out through a double French door we have on the back of the house. I had a terrific battle against the current but finally opened wide the doors and pulled the dining room table between them to keep them open and the whirling black mass swept out. However the rooms were all flooded by that time, but that kept the pressure from tearing out the rear walls as the sediment and boulders piled up. All that happened in split seconds. I heard Bobby cry out and I waded back into the bedroom where he had fallen out into the whirling waters. I picked him out and tossed him onto the bed. Skippy the dog bounded in and onto the bed with him. I then boosted Hazel up into the clothes closet where a 3 foot hole opened up into the attic. Then I handed Bobby to her and then the dog.

Next I waded into the back bedroom where grandma had run and I carried her through the muck and pushed her up into the attic. Then Mr. Harbin and I carried the crippled wife into the attic, also her parrot and cat she had brought along. Then Harbin and I started cleaning out the clothes closets of dry coats and wraps and bedding and shoved them into the attic where Hazel took them and wrapped Bobby and the others in as we were in our pajamas. I took the two mattresses and by super human effort squeezed them through the attic. All this time the water was rising and as I watched the black stuff creeping up, I began to wonder what my experience was going to be like while drowning in that thick stuff. I didn't think we had a ghost of a chance and fully expected to be destroyed but know I must keep taking advantage of every little thing I could think of. Afterwards I found I had even taken a half pitcher of water we had sitting on the buffet up into the attic as I know we would be a long time without water maybe. And the only eatable I could grab was a can of popcorn balls. All this time the house was surrounded by a raging torrent of water. Great boulders were hitting the front of the house. Windows were crashing in. A full sized barrel came plunging into the front room. The paving came in chunks. Parts of trees were swirling in the front room. The front door was piled high with debris. Boulders as high as our car we found out at daylight were crashing by. Our yard is full of them, all sizes. I looked out the attic window and into the torrent. A woman screamed and yelled for help as she was sweeping by. She disappeared in a second. A garage man was swept out of his home two blocks above us along with his garage and rode the waves and grabbed onto a telephone pole just 75 feet west of the house. He clung there for an hour and a half he later said. His hand was crushed.

When the waters began to subside I decided to reach the two boys in case they were still alive. I waded to the neighbor's back porch, flashed my light and called out. No answer. I went to the front door and called out. No answer. I waded in through their front room and called out. No answer. I felt sure they had been washed away. I went into the bedroom and flashed my light. The beds were floating but no life. I called once more in desperation and like music from the heavens a voice answered. The two boys and the couple, Mr. and Mrs. Davis, were huddled up in a four foot attic. They were cold and in wet nighties. I carried the boys over one at a time on my back and shoved them into the attic. And that was Hazel's big moment when she reached out for the two boys. The young couple came up too as we decided their house would soon be undermined and fall into a deep channel that was eating its way toward the house. We all spent the rest of the night in our attic. Ten people, three puppies and their bulldog mother, our dog Skippy, a parrot, a cat and our two lovebirds. Our lovebirds were always kept in the front room on a floor stand. I didn't expect that they had survived but when I took a look they were right where they had always stood and were safe. But the piano had been swung around in the room. Your picture, Mother, was still upright on the piano. The davenport

The three Crowe boys across from their house on Prospect Avenue, where they had sheltered overnight in the attic with seven other people and their pets. The tall house is the Crowes' and the house next door is the Davises'. The Crowe house still stands, relatively unchanged. *Courtesy of Bob Crowe.*

was floating amidst the debris. The west wall of the sun room buckled out and left a gaping hole near the floor where boulders had crashed through, and the boy's toys and Christmas tree had swept out. Kirk's violin and my saxophone and clarinet were swept out and down the valley probably under tons of dirt now. The piano is ruined I think. Everything really needs replacing but we dug it out and 15 of the letter carriers came up last Sat. and carried everything into a house we have now rented until we can recover and get squared around.

We are only one family in hundreds that have been swept out. I could tell you of scenes and heart breaking stories and death dramas that would turn your blood cold. So many families broken up. Parts of families missing or children being dug up way down in Glendale, who were swept out of their tiny beds up here in La Crescenta eight miles away. Two legs of an eight year old girl were found. A father with a broken back and four of his five children swept away. Cars being entirely covered with sand with their occupants inside. A big beer garden with 500 autos covered. Rescuers digging out the bodies still settling in their chairs at the table celebrating

New Year's. Houses completely swept away into kindling wood. Someone's bathtub is sitting in our front yard. A piano swept out of one house and into another. The newspaper death list gives around 40, but one day alone there were 200 bodies in one little mortuary. 17 Red Cross women being trapped in the basement of the American Legion Hall. I found a twenty inch petrified bone of a large animal under our piano when I dug it out. A large tusk of a prehistoric animal was dug out of the sand down the street, which was swept down from the mountains. Hundreds of cars demolished along the streets completely covered. Nearly all bridges out. Glendale business section flooded. The three folks who came over to our house to spend the night, went back to their home the next morning and there wasn't over a quart of water in the house and it was only 150 feet from our house.

With Love and Best Wishes, Charlie, Letter Carrier 47, Glendale, Calif.

The following account was written based on an interview with Bob Lorenz. It was published recently in the Crescenta Valley Weekly:

In 1933 the Lorenz family had a home at the top of Briggs Avenue. Even back then, there were a good number of homes tucked way up on a flat area called Briggs Terrace at the mouth of Pickens Canyon. In November of that year a massive fire broke out on the front face of the mountains above the Lorenz home, but wind drove the fire northwest toward Tujunga. In the middle of the night, the fire's direction reversed and came roaring back down Pickens Canyon to quickly burn several of the Briggs Terrace homes, including the Lorenz house. Bob Lorenz, just 11 years old then, remembers being hustled out of bed at 2:00 AM just ahead of the firestorm. The flames were so close, that as the family fled, Bob's mother had to extinguish the sparks that were landing on his clothes.

The Lorenz family had lost everything, and moved in with the Grandparents down in LA. A month later, just after Christmas, they were missing their old neighbors up on the Terrace, so they decided to drive up and spend the evening visiting in their old neighborhood. The night they chose was, unfortunately, New Year's Eve. Unbeknownst to them, they were headed into a disaster zone again.

Despite heavy rain, the family caravanned up in two cars, and spent a pleasant evening staying dry and warm with old neighbors. Just before midnight, there was a massive cloudburst, and a few minutes later as they

The Bluebird Diner on Pennsylvania Avenue. The man who owned the diner lost his house in the flood, so he closed the restaurant and converted it into a home for his family, as shown here. This building, much modified and hardly recognizable, still exists near the corner of Pennsylvania and Honolulu. *Courtesy of Kathryn Halford.*

toasted the New Year, the ground began to shake. They listened in terror as what sounded like a fast freight train roared past them. That was the sound of thousands of tons of boulders and logs headed down Pickens Canyon. For the Lorenz family, it was time to get out.

In their two cars, Mom driving one, and Dad the other, they headed back down Briggs. When they hit Foothill, where a 20-foot high wall of fast moving water, rocks and mud had jumped out of the canyon's channel and spread, they found La Crescenta unrecognizable. Streets and buildings were gone, and massive car-sized boulders were scattered everywhere. They continued downhill through deep water, over rocks and mud, and at some point the two cars got separated.

In Mom's car, they were told by a rescue worker to head to the American Legion Hall where the Red Cross had set up a refugee station. Little did they know that the Legion Hall had already been hit by the flood, and that the Red Cross workers and many of the refugees were now dead. They slogged along Montrose Avenue, but finally sank into deep mud and spent the night cold, wet and terrified in the car.

Meanwhile Dad's car, with Bob inside, had picked its way west across the wrecked landscape below Montrose Avenue. They had given up getting out of the valley, and instead were attempting to reach a friend's house on the west side. They had turned uphill at Pennsylvania, but finally bogged down in front of the Bluebird Diner at Pennsylvania and Honolulu. The waiters waved them inside, and they spent the night inside the restaurant. Incidentally, that diner is still there, now a little non-descript office/retail place at 3971 Pennsylvania.

The Lorenz family survived, and rebuilt up on Briggs Terrace, and Bob Lorenz, proud to call himself a flood survivor, has lived here ever since.

An excerpt of a letter written by Sister Achala of the Ananda Ashrama on January 16:

When they returned to check the temple patio, they saw a water fall coming down the temple steps going up to temple hill. Swamiji ran up through the water to his study door where he expected that it had forced its way inside. At that moment, there came such a tremendous roar that it was almost deafening. In a few seconds, when Jessie and Sister Amala came up, he tried to make Jessie hear him. She was only 30 feet away, but she couldn't understand what he was telling her. He asked her to stand on the rug barricading his study door. Sister Amala yelled that water was being forced into the temple from the other arcade. He sent her down to find anything she could to block the temple door and to get some of the men to come up to help. She brought another rug and stood on it. The electricity was out and they worked furiously by flashlight.

Then, the flood water began to flow through the temple arcade like a raging river. Swamiji had no tools with him, so he used his legs to try to prevent the accumulation of debris, sand, rocks, stones from piling up. Then, he took the longest chime to try to disperse as much debris as possible to make a water way. They later learned that a cloudburst had taken place.

By the time George, Lama Carlson, Mr. Garman and others from the community arrived, they were panic stricken that they had been outside in the cloudburst. Those who had remained in the cloister had witnessed what appeared to be lightning, but it was really the high-tension electrical wires which had gone down making flashes across the sky. The roar, they learned afterwards, was the flash flood roaring down Dunsmore Canyon which adjoins the Ashrama property line on the west.

George took Swamiji up towards the bee house, the upper cabins and towards Dunsmore Canyon. The wide gap between the Ashrama and the Le Mesnager property—100 feet wide—was a roaring, raging river and through it came down upon New York Avenue boulders and giant trees. They walked carefully over the demolished electrical poles and fallen electrical wires. What they saw made their hearts sink. The little brown house that stood at the top of New York Avenue, occupied by Professor McIntyre, his wife and little baby, was gone. All that was left was a portion of the chimney.

Monday, January 1ˢᵗ, the New Year had already started. It was about 1 AM. There was no water running through the pipes in the house because the great big water pipes coming down from Dunsmore Canyon were twisted and broken like small pieces of wire.

Swamiji suggested having their New Year's Eve service. It was the most unique and memorable service they had ever had. Immediately after the service, Swamiji had a peculiar feeling of depression about the valley. They were safe, but he and community felt so ominous about the people in the valley...as if they had heard a cry of distress.

It was about 3 AM on Monday, January 1ˢᵗ when they retired. He told everyone to sleep in and that they wouldn't have their usual 7:30 AM service until later. However, at about 6 AM, Swamiji had a peculiar feeling that all wasn't right at the temple. When he got up there, he discovered that everything seemed changed: the contour of the hills, the levels of the temple grounds.

An excerpt of a letter written by Sister Amala of the Ananda Ashrama on January 16:

Mr. Reihl wept as he told them how, after midnight as he and his wife, Ruth, wished each other "Happy New Year," their house was struck a terrific blow by boulders and water. As she was swept from him, he heard her say, "O my God!" Then, he was shot through the wall of his house through a hole made by the water. His legs and arms were scratched by the metal wiring used for holding stucco. He was carried for two blocks, trying to catch the tops of oak trees on his rapid journey, but the current made it impossible. He landed on some boulders and was washed up onto the steps of a house. The man who dragged him into the house didn't know whether it was a person or a dog. After bathing the sand and dirt off his face, he recognized an old friend, Sergeant Reihl...and Mr. Reihl looked up into the face of Colonel May! Both had been in the war together.

From 3 AM until 11 AM, Mr. Reihl searched for the body of his wife. It was when he was in the Fire House that Ruth appeared to him and pointed toward their home. There, in the wreckage he found her body. He collapsed and at 4 PM, he finally received first aid for injuries received 16 hours earlier.

Mary Darrow, a reporter for the Crescenta Valley Ledger, *gave an eyewitness account of life in the disaster area:*

La Crescenta and Montrose Residents Hear Strange Remarks as Throng Pokes Way Through Ruins; Guards Accommodate Seekers of Thrills

At the Verdugo Legion Hall where two workers lost their lives and where to prevent curiosity hunters from entering the damaged hall, the holes have been boarded up. "Why there's only one hole here, they told me it was absolutely a wreck."

At a private home, "Look, why they're living here. How do they do it?" At another home a woman peering into the windows remarks: "Nothing to see here, the furniture is gone."

Guards at the street entrances to the stricken area are getting a thrill out of giving a thrill to the thrill seekers. For instance: "Yes'm, they smothered to death, I guess." Still another: "Oh yes, the men working here say they take out bodies every day, but they won't let them tell where they get them or what is done with them."

At a distribution center for clothes for the needy: "I like this dress and the way it's made, but really, my dear, you know I couldn't wear this color with my complexion. Won't you see if you can find one like it in another color?" Another one hunting a winter coat, after going over the entire stock: "I don't seem to find just what I want. Yes, I know they're warm, but I really like fur on my winter coat."

Stealing, oh my yes, property owners have to literally sit on their possessions. Washings on the clothes lines are not safe, according to reports of irate housewives. Many of the houses have two paid guards sitting on the steps to protect them against trespassers.

Up and down the roads in the stricken area go the patient burros carrying the water buckets for the CWA men who are cleaning houses and clearing up lots. One of these workers, "Rastus," a Negro, says he gets up at 3 a.m. every day to walk from Los Angeles to work here. Once in a while he is able to get a ride.

Steam shovels and ditch diggers clearing roads, and wrecks of autos are still being found under tons of mud. At night, camp fires of the sentinels at each entrance to the devastated area give an eerie glow to the scene.

Articles including a child's bathing suit, a shoe, keys, empty pocketbooks, cups from a soda fountain, smashed fiddles, all are found in the claim department under the direction of the Sheriff's office. Shoes, underwear and other garments being given out so that the man of the family may

Shovel men formed lines to "sweep" streets of debris.

go out to work and keep comfortable. Lines of refugees seeking to be rehabilitated, answering questions, begging for help—cheerful workers giving all the aid possible.

And over all the California sunshine is giving a note of cheerfulness and lending encouragement to the flood sufferers who are carrying on.

This is the text of a speech given at the La Crescenta Woman's Club recently by flood survivor Eloise Benson Nicholl:

In November 1933 there was a major fire in our foothills. Everything burned. The hills were denuded. The week before the flood, we had rain every day. The CCC had constructed check dams—wire and rocks—in Pickens Canyon above Foothill. That's all the protection there was.

I was just a little girl but I remember well the growing premonition I had that week that something terrible was going to happen. Around 10 p.m. on New Year's Eve, the little dams could hold no more water and they let loose.

I'm not sure how we knew that—by radio, I suppose. Anyway, I decided that this was what I had been fearing. Relieved, I went to bed.

Then at midnight, the real flood came. Not everyone agrees on the time as flood waters came down from several canyons. My brother, Malcolm Benson, remembers it to have been at midnight exactly as he was boiling water for his tea, and the flood hit just as the teakettle started to whistle.

Anyway, we heard it coming, a very loud roar. We huddled in the dining room, looking out the window. Mother knocked over a standing planter and she hastened to clean up the mess. I wondered why—I had a sense that we soon would be washed away.

We watched as the second house to the east of us washed across the street and was deposited in their front yard. The house next to us filled up to the window sills with adobe-type mud which hardened. We decided that we had been spared because our house was a foot higher. Our neighbor, Mr. Broun, stayed with us. His wife left to stay with her brother as she had a job with the telephone company. Mr. Broun literally had to chisel out the adobe from each inch of each room.

Many houses were left intact but were filled with two to three feet of mud. Even today, in some older homes, dirt is found inside walls and behind cabinets during home renovations.

Our home was 1½ blocks south of Foothill and the water that rushed past us destroyed the American Legion Hall, five or six streets directly below us.

Refugees had been taken to the Legion Hall. Assisting those who had been injured was Dr. Vera Kahn. She was among the dozen or so who lost their lives. Dr. Kahn was a member of this Club. Also she and my mother, Ruth Benson, were members of the American Legion Glee Club. Dressed in white, Glee Club members stood in two rows as her casket was carried into St. Luke's of the Mountains Church. As the casket passed, each Glee Club member dropped a white gardenia on it. During the services, the Glee Club sang "Beautiful Isle of Somewhere." It was a very sobering occasion. Dr. Kahn is buried in Arlington National Cemetery next to her husband who was lost in WWI.

My brother's Boy Scout troop used to meet at the Legion Hall. The room was destroyed. Malcolm wrote to his teacher:

"Dear Mr. Morgan:

The Boy Scouts (Montrose No. 2) are selling these folders at 25¢ each in order to get a fresh start after the flood, where all of their flags and equipment were washed away. I am leaving one in your box, and if you wish to buy it, please leave the money with Miss Brown, my Mother or me. If you don't care for it, please put the folder in my Mother's box. There are 26 pictures of the flood.

Thank you, Malcolm Benson"

The whole area was several feet higher than normal as the silt hardened. Malcolm and I walked to Montrose, across the devastated area. So many homes were missing; so many cars were strewn about, stuck in the mud. There were many things sticking up in the hardened silt. One precious thing found was a silver server with the Van Deusen's initials embossed on it. Mrs. Van Deusen was President of the Club that year. There were other personal things: Bibles, books, pictures, even a piano. On Sundays, people drove out from Los Angeles to view the destruction. They were permitted to come up Verdugo to Ocean View to Foothill then down La Crescenta Avenue. They were directed by the police and were not permitted to stop.

Our Club was 23 years old that year. There was a New Year's Eve dance going on that evening and when the refugees began arriving, they were told that it was a private party. They were informed that the private party was over, that the Club would be used for a hospital from now on, and maybe even a morgue. The injured were cared for by the Red Cross until they could

AMERICAN LEGION

Verdugo Hills Post 288

SOUVENIR FOLDER

OF

MONTROSE - LA CRESCENTA FLOOD
NEW YEAR'S DAY, 1934

Proceeds from sale of this book will be used to help rebuild Legion Club House and Boy Scout Club Room, Troop No. 2.

Photographs by
ARTHUR C. OSTERMANN
MONTROSE, CALIFORNIA

Printed by
GLENDALE PRINTERS
216 SO. BRAND, GLENDALE

Souvenir photo books like this were quickly printed after the flood to sell to the thousands of curious sightseers who flocked to the valley to view the destruction. The profits went to community groups that had been impacted by the disaster, in this case the American Legion and the Boy Scout troop that shared the Legion Hall.

be taken to hospitals. The Club was also a distribution center for clothing. There were so many who had lost everything; so many were homeless. The homeless were fed—some 400–500 every 24 hours. Money, food and clothing were sent from Woman's Clubs from all over this section of the country.

No wonder the journalist wrote for the local paper: "If the La Crescenta Woman's Club has never done anything in the past and was never to do anything in the future, it has done sufficient in this emergency to assure its niche in the local Hall of Fame." He ends, "It will remain open until the present need is entirely passed."

We can indeed be proud of the heroic efforts of our Club's predecessors.

This is an excerpt from a recent column in the Crescenta Valley Weekly *about the fate of the Doty twins:*

Weston and Winston Doty were born into an acting family, and so naturally, as cute and charming identical twin boys, they were drafted into filmmaking at a young age. They made several Hal Roach "Our Gang" shorts, the most successful being 1922's "One Terrible Day" in which the twins spoke and moved in unison. They played twin Lost Boys in a 1924 production of "Peter Pan," starring Betty Bronson. They also had successful radio careers, but their biggest fame came later in life as twin cheerleaders for the USC Trojans in 1931 and 32. It was said people attended the games as much to see the handsome, vivacious young performers as to watch the actual football game.

These two celebrities and their dates had driven up from Venice to be the guests of honor at a New Year's Eve Party at the home of Henry Hesse at 2631 Manhattan Ave. in Montrose. The main topic of conversation that Dec. 31st night was the Rose Bowl game the following day between Stanford and Columbia, but a background topic was the weather. A Pacific storm series had been hitting the Crescenta Valley hard for the previous two weeks, and the burned off San Gabriel Mountains had been shedding water and mud all that day, flooding some homes. A Red Cross evacuation center had been set up at the America Legion Hall just a couple of blocks away, and displaced residents were already gathering there. At midnight at the Hesse house the Doty Twins made a call to their mother to wish her a happy new year, the last she would ever hear from them. As soon as they hung up the phone, Mr. Hesse heard rumbling and water noise outside. Looking out the back door, he saw the back porch ripped from the house. He shouted,

"Everyone get out!" grabbed his wife, and ran for the front door. The guests poured out onto the front porch as the house collapsed behind them, and jumped into several feet of swirling water and mud. Hesse and his wife grabbed a tree trunk floating by and rode it several blocks until it lodged against a wall, where they spent the night astride the log. The majority of the guests at the party were killed, including the twins. The bodies of the 19-year-old boys were later found close to each other amongst the debris in Verdugo Canyon.

They were interred together at Woodlawn Cemetery in Santa Monica. The following year, their grief-stricken father died alone in a Chicago hotel room of a heart attack.

A drive by 2631 Manhattan today is telling. There is no 2631. The Pickens Flood Control Channel occupies that address.

The following is an excerpt from a recent letter written by flood survivor Dick Lamar:

Although I was only 12 at the time, I vividly remember the flood of 1934. My father was the commander of the American Legion Post at the time. He and Myrtle Adams were standing on the front porch of the Legion Hall when they heard the flood waters rushing down from the hills to the north. The sound was deafening. My father had a brief second to leap up into the branches of a sycamore tree next to the porch. The flood waters washed out the back of the building onto the porch and Ms. Adams was swept away. My father survived and finally made it home by walking several blocks in the dark.

Later that morning a very elderly woman knocked on our door. Her house had been lifted up from its foundation and over a row of cypress trees and finally came to rest against a telephone pole on Montrose Ave.—several blocks west of our home. She kept covering her mouth with her hand and seemed very embarrassed. She said that she had put her dentures in a glass of water on top of the toilet bowl. Could we possibly go back to her wrecked house and search for her dentures. It seemed like a long shot, but my father and I set out for her home and found it up against the telephone pole and cocked at a crazy angle. Managed to climb in, found the bathroom and there were her dentures in the glass of water teetering at a 30 degree angle. It seemed like a miracle.

This is the front porch of the American Legion Hall, where Tob Lamar and Myrtle Adams were standing when the flood hit. Lamar was able to leap into the tree on the right as the flood passed below him. Adams was swept away and killed. That sycamore tree still stands next to the house that was built over the site of the Legion Hall at Fairway and Rosemont.

This house floated intact down Del Mar Avenue and came to rest against this telephone pole on the southwest corner of Orangedale and Montrose Avenue, across from Holy Redeemer Church. It was in the bathroom of this house that Dick Lamar found the unspilled glass of water containing the old lady's dentures. The telephone pole is still there; the house is not.

This account is from an unknown newspaper clipping:

J.A. Paschall of La Crescenta had a queer experience on New Year's Eve. His home off Briggs avenue is very near Pickens canyon and he told how the boulders, many weighing twenty tons or more, rolled down the wash to the accompaniment of the roar of the waters. He stated the first heavy flow of water came at 9:30 and his home shook as though it were in the grasp of an earthquake. In fact more than it did during an earthquake. His cement porch floor was cracked and the plaster in his home was also cracked as the result of the vibration of the boulders as they smashed against each other.

This account is from an unknown newspaper clipping:

On New Year's Eve both A.E. Baron and Mr. Poole had broadcast from Verdugo Hills post American Legion hall telling about conditions in the valley and that a temporary headquarters for the American Red Cross had been established in the hall where shelter and care could be found. There were many volunteers for service and thirteen refugees came to the hall for shelter. At 10 o'clock when waters were surrounding the hall Mr. Poole advised removal but the women feared the rocks, twice the size of a bushel basket, then rolling down Rosemont Avenue, would wreck the cars.

About 12 o'clock the second cloudburst occurred just as Mr. Poole was leaving the phone. When the back wall of the building went out things happened rapidly. He remembered seeing the piano tip backwards and then start for the front door. Mr. Poole was making his way to Mrs. Adams when he was caught by the wall of water that tumbled and rolled him about until he reached Montrose Avenue where he caught onto a bush. Having been completely covered in water he heard no cries of distress. He was mired in silt up to his armpits and his mouth being full of gravel made him unable to call. Gradually he made his way to a stump in the middle of the street and there he clung until three boys from a nearby stalled car came to his rescue and carried him to Miss Reno's real estate office.

An ambulance took him to the hospital. Mr. Poole suffered a broken shoulder, four broken ribs, an injured back and many bruises. Three infections resulted, one in the right eye. It took three days to free his mouth of gravel.

Longtime resident Don Norbut had an uncle, Harry Pulfer, who lived up in Big Tujunga Canyon in 1933. This is an excerpt of a recent interview with Don:

The Big Tujunga Wash was covered mountain to mountain. It was solid water from this hillside to that hillside. So what they did is—do you know what a breeches buoy is? They shot a line over the top of the water, from one side to the other, and they put a basket on the line. They put the people in the basket, and they pulled the people across. And that's how they got my family out of there. They put them in there and hauled them over to the other side, hand over hand, with that breeches buoy. And they had horses there, and the horses took them out. There was quite a community up there. They had about four or five houses up there. And they all had to be taken out this way.

The editorial page of the Crescenta Valley Ledger *indulged in a bit of local boosterism after the flood with the following piece:*

"Who's afraid of the big, bad flood!"

Certainly not the eighteen new families who moved into the Crescenta valley last week!

They say figures don't lie—and that's the actual check-up results for last week. I'm not going to say that this indicates the rapid "comeback" being staged by the valley. That would be untrue—it never lost out. True, there were quite a number of families who left these parts immediately after the flood, but—a check-up on the public utility records will show that they too are beginning to return.

Don't let anyone fool you, mister, after we once get a taste of the valley we just can't leave it—for long.

The writer KNOWS

HE TRIED IT!

A few residents were opposed to the debris basin concept as evidenced by this article from the Crescenta Valley Ledger *on February 11, 1934:*

ANTI-DEBRIS BASIN GROUP WILL MEET; OBJECTIONS SEEN

Further objections to the proposed construction of the debris basins at the foot of the Sierras as a means of combating the flood menace, is expected to develop this evening at a meeting of the North Briggs Avenue Property Owners' association, scheduled to be held at the office of N.W. Zimmer, 2611 Foothill boulevard.

The association strongly opposes the construction of a debris basin in what is termed one of the finest residential sections in the valley. The organization is strong in its conviction that the building of proper check dams, reforestation and other methods of flood control is the solution of the problem.

Its officers claim the debris basin construction would prove a waste of the taxpayers' money, and would prove a menace to life and health. A record turnout is expected at tonight's meeting.

The Crescenta Valley Ledger, *December 1935, nearly a year after the flood:*

Xmas Happiness Marred by Death

Christmas will not be a time of merriment and happiness at the Harry Wilson home in La Crescenta. Instead of Santa Claus, the Angel of Death appeared at this season and carried away Marddie Marie Wilson to join her sister and two brothers who were lost in the New Year 1934 flood.

The fourteen year old girl has been ill since she was swept away with her family when their home collapsed and they were at the mercy of the storm. Her sister's body was found in Glendale and those of the two brothers somewhat near where their home had been. Mr. Wilson had his back broken during that harrowing night and his wife, too, was hurt. One child was unharmed.

Valiantly Marddie fought for her life since that time and for a while it seemed that blindness would also be her portion. She died on Tuesday at General Hospital, five days after she had passed her fourteenth birthday.

Funeral services will be held today.

From a column in the Crescenta Valley Weekly. *This is a reminder that physical relics of the tragedy are still with us in our daily lives:*

Death Once Stalked Our American Legion Hall

The Verdugo Hills Memorial Hall located at 4011 La Crescenta Avenue serves as the home for local American Legion Post 288 and the Veterans of Foreign Wars. It also hosts church groups, exercise classes, and Boy Scout meetings. But unbeknownst to most, this hall was the site of swift and powerful violence that took the lives of at least 12 men, women and children, and injured many more. Perhaps the word "Memorial" in the hall's title should give us a clue that the quiet Legion Hall was once a death trap.

Here's the story behind this recently re-discovered revelation. In the 1920's the Crescenta Valley was booming, and hundreds, including many WWI veterans, moved here to take advantage of our beautiful climate. An American Legion Hall was built on the corner of Rosemont and Fairway Avenue to serve the growing town, as both a home for newly formed Legion Post 288 and as a community center. In October of 1925 the Crescenta Valley celebrated its dedication with huge fanfare and speeches by dignitaries. It served the community faithfully for nearly a decade, no one knowing that it had been built in the destructive path of the geologically regular flash floods that swept the valley a couple of times each century.

In late 1933 a destructive fire cleared the front range of the San Gabriel Mountains of vegetation, and heavy rains through December generated mud flows. By December 31st the Legion Hall had been set up as a Red Cross evacuation center for those whose homes had been flooded. American Legion Auxiliary members Myrtle Adams and Dr. Vera Kahn were in charge as dozens of refugees crowded into the hall, and the word went out across the Valley to head for the Legion Hall for safety.

At midnight on New Years Eve of 1934, a huge cloudburst hit the rain soaked hillsides above our valley, and the mud and rocks cut loose and roared down the canyons. The 20 foot high debris flow, a slurry of mud and rocks with massive boulders being pushed in front, flew down Pickens Canyon at about 30 mph, crossed Foothill Boulevard and tore through the populated areas above the Legion Hall. The debris flow clipped the edge of the hall, knocking the back wall in. The interior of the hall filled quickly with a mud and rock mixture, which swirled a bit, crushing the occupants against the walls, and then punched a hole in the front wall and exited, carrying all inside with it. At least 12 of the refugees, including Mrs. Adams and Dr. Kahn, were dead, and scores were injured. Overall the flood killed scores and left hundreds homeless.

The Crescenta Valley was a place of great resilience back then, and the community immediately started rebuilding, including making plans for a new American Legion Hall. The Bonetto Family who lived on

Sightseers walk around the American Legion Hall the day after the flood. Although the majority of deaths occurred in this building, the photo shows that it was amazingly undamaged. The shot is from Rosemont looking east.

Manhattan Avenue near La Crescenta Avenue donated land for a new Hall, and by July, steam shovels began excavating the new site.

The old Legion Hall on Rosemont, although it had a big hole in both the front and back, was still standing. It being the Great Depression, money and materials were tight. The decision was made to reuse the building, and it was jacked up off its foundation, and set down on wheels. An *LA Times* photo from August of '34 shows the intact building being towed down Montrose Ave. by a pitifully small truck. It was set in place on its new basement foundation on La Crescenta Avenue in a reversed position, with the old front of the hall facing the rear of the property. Twelve feet of new building, now the entry and offices, was added on the La Crescenta Avenue side. The labor and materials to finish it were donated by the community, and the hall was rededicated as a memorial to Adams and Kahn.

A community eager to put a tragic past behind it quickly forgot that this was the same building that had once been the site of a deadly natural disaster, and for decades now, no one has considered the ghosts of those who died there.

SUGGESTED READING

Bailey, Thomas, and David Kennedy. *The American Pageant*. Lexington, MA: D.C. Heath and Company, 1983.

Bean, Walton. *California: An Interpretation*. N.p.: McGraw Hill Book Company, 1968.

Boucher, David. *Ride the Devil Wind*. Bellflower, CA: Fire Publications, 1991.

Chawner, W.D. "The Montrose–La Crescenta (CA) Flood of January 1, 1934." Master's thesis, Balch Graduate School, California Institute of Technology, Pasadena, CA, 1934.

Crescenta Valley Ledger, 1925–1978. Microfilm Collection, Glendale Central Library, Glendale, CA.

Dougherty, June. *Sources of History*. Distributed by June Dougherty, 1993.

Gumprecht, Blake. *The Los Angeles River: Its Life, Death, and Possible Rebirth*. Baltimore, MD: Johns Hopkins, 2001.

McPhee, John. *The Control of Nature*. New York: Noonday Press, Farrar, Straus and Giroux, 1997.

Morrison, Patt. *Rio L.A.: Tales from the Los Angeles River*. Photographs by Mark Lamonica. Santa Monica, CA: Angel Press, 2001.

Oberbeck, Grace. *History of the La Crescenta-La Cañada Valleys*. Montrose, CA: The Ledger, 1938.

Robinson, John W., with Doug Christiansen. *Trails of the Angelus*. Berkeley, CA: Wilderness Press, 2005.

Rolle, Andrew F. *California: A History*. New York: Thomas Y. Crowell Company, 1963.

Taylor, Nick. *The Enduring Legacy of the W.P.A.: American-Made, When F.D.R. Put the Nation to Work*. N.p.: Bantam Books, 2008.

Troxell, Harold, and John Peterson. *Flood in La Cañada Valley, CA, January 1, 1934*. Geological Survey. Washington, D.C.: United States Printing Office, 1937.

INDEX

ABOUT THE AUTHORS

A rt Cobery taught United States history at Burbank High School for over three decades. He retired in 1989. Prior to becoming a founding member of the Historical Society of the Crescenta Valley, he devoted his energies to preserving the *Crescenta Valley Ledger* on microfilm. While engaged in this endeavor, he became fascinated by the paper's forgotten stories relating to the Crescenta Valley Flood of 1934.

M ike Lawler is the president of the Historical Society of the Crescenta Valley. He produces a weekly "Treasures of the Valley" column and writes captions for a weekly photo feature, "Crescenta Valley Then and Now," in the *Crescenta Valley Weekly*.

P am Lawler, a third-generation Glendalian who grew up with the stories of the flood as seen by her mother in 1934, first met Art Cobery as her "favorite" U.S. history teacher in high school.